Know your furniture parts.
Here's how it all comes together.

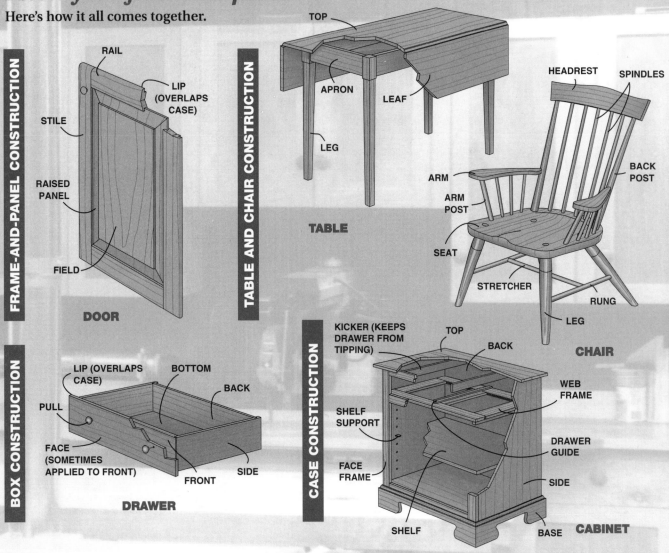

FRAME-AND-PANEL CONSTRUCTION

RAIL
LIP (OVERLAPS CASE)
STILE
RAISED PANEL
FIELD

DOOR

TABLE AND CHAIR CONSTRUCTION

TOP
APRON
LEAF
LEG

TABLE

HEADREST
SPINDLES
ARM
ARM POST
BACK POST
SEAT
STRETCHER
RUNG
LEG

CHAIR

BOX CONSTRUCTION

LIP (OVERLAPS CASE)
PULL
FACE (SOMETIMES APPLIED TO FRONT)
BOTTOM
BACK
FRONT
SIDE

DRAWER

CASE CONSTRUCTION

KICKER (KEEPS DRAWER FROM TIPPING)
TOP
BACK
WEB FRAME
SHELF SUPPORT
DRAWER GUIDE
FACE FRAME
SIDE
SHELF
BASE

CABINET

Know your decorative shapes.
These are the elements of woodworking style.

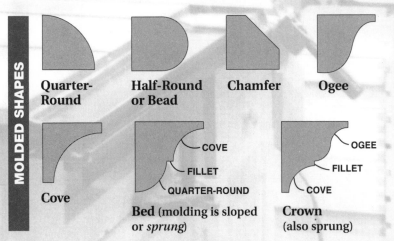

MOLDED SHAPES

Quarter-Round

Half-Round or Bead

Chamfer

Ogee

Cove

COVE
FILLET
QUARTER-ROUND

Bed (molding is sloped or *sprung*)

OGEE
FILLET
COVE

Crown (also sprung)

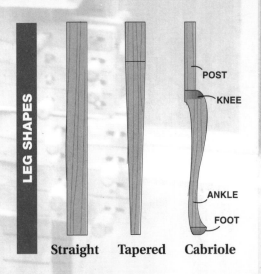

LEG SHAPES

POST
KNEE
ANKLE
FOOT

Straight   **Tapered**   **Cabriole**

Secrets of Successful Woodworking™

Making Flawless Cabinets and Built-ins

MAKING FLAWLESS CABINETS AND BUILT-INS

Nick Engler

Rodale Press, Inc.
Emmaus, Pennsylvania

OUR PURPOSE

"We inspire and enable people to improve their lives and the world around them."

Bookworks Staff
Designer: Linda Watts
Illustrator and Project Designer: Mary Jane Favorite
Art assistance: David Van Etten
Interior and Back Cover Photographer: Karen Callahan
Master Craftsman: Jim McCann

Rodale Press Home and Garden Books Staff
Vice President and Editorial Director: Margaret J. Lydic
Managing Editor, Woodworking Books: Rick Peters
Editor: Tony O'Malley
Director of Design and Production: Michael Ward
Associate Art Director: Carol Angstadt
Cover Designer and design assistance: Dale Mack
Front Cover Photographer: Mitch Mandel
Studio Manager: Leslie M. Keefe
Copy Director: Dolores Plikaitis
Copy Editors: Sara Cox and Barbara McIntosh Webb
Book Manufacturing Director: Helen Clogston
Manufacturing Coordinator: Patrick T. Smith
Office Manager: Karen Earl-Braymer
Editorial assistance: Jodi Guiducci

Special Thanks to:
Rich and Susan Burmann
Eaton, Ohio

Glen and Jan Cox
Dayton, Ohio

Curry's Video Plus
West Milton, Ohio

Daniel Garber
Clayton, Ohio

Chris Walendzak
Centerville, Ohio

Wertz Stores
West Milton, Ohio

Workshops of David T. Smith
Morrow, Ohio

© 1998 by Bookworks, Inc.
Published by Rodale Press, Inc.
By arrangement with Bookworks, Inc.

The author and editors who compiled this book have tried to make all of the contents as accurate and as correct as possible. Plans, illustrations, photographs, and text have all been carefully checked and cross-checked. However, due to the variability of local conditions, construction materials, personal skill, and so on, neither the author nor Rodale Press assumes any responsibility for any injuries suffered or for damages or other losses incurred that result from the material presented herein. All instructions and plans should be carefully studied and clearly understood before beginning construction.

Printed in the United States of America on acid-free ∞, recycled ♻ paper

Library of Congress Cataloging-in-Publication Data

Engler, Nick.
    Making flawless cabinets and built-ins /
Nick Engler.
        p.   cm.   (Secrets of successful
woodworking ; #1)
    Includes bibliographical references and index.
    ISBN 0–87596–805–8   (hardcover)
    1. Woodwork.   2. Cabinetwork.   3. Built-in
furniture.   I. Title.   II. Series: Engler, Nick. Secrets of
successful woodworking ; #1.
    TT180 .E645   1998
    684.1'6—ddc21   98–8912

Distributed in the book trade by St. Martin's Press

2 4 6 8 10 9 7 5 3 1   hardcover

We're always happy to hear from you. For questions or comments concerning the editorial content of this book, please write to:
    Rodale Press, Inc.
    Book Readers' Service
    33 East Minor Street
    Emmaus, PA 18098

Look for other Rodale books wherever books are sold. Or call us at (800) 848-4735.

For more information about Rodale Press and the books and magazines we publish, visit our World Wide Web site at:
    http://www.rodalepress.com

Cabinetmaking: Exploring the Possibilities

There are few woodworking projects that present as many possibilities as a cabinet. At its heart, it's nothing more than an enclosed space with a door. But you can build this enclosure to any size or shape, fill it with any number of shelves and drawers, enclose it with solid doors to hide its contents or glass doors to display them, decorate it with moldings and appliqués, raise it up on a base, then top it off with a pediment or a bonnet.

I've written this book to help you explore all of these possibilities. This is not just a *techniques* book, although it explains all major cabinetmaking methods. And it's not just a *project* book, although there are complete plans and instructions for building five handsome cabinets. It's not an *idea* book, although you'll find photographs for many different styles of cabinets built by accomplished craftsmen from all over America. It's not a *jigs and fixtures* book, although you'll find plenty of them. It's *all of these* — and something completely different.

What you have here are blow-by-blow descriptions of what it took for a band of craftsmen to build the five cabinet projects shown here — not just what we did but also the problems we came up against and how we solved them.

Making Flawless Cabinets and Built-ins starts out with a simple cabinet, the **Spice Cupboard.** This shows you how to assemble a cabinet case, make adjustable shelves, and hang a frame-and-panel door. With the **Mission Bookcase,** we cover two other important cabinetmaking ingredients — a face frame and glazed doors. The **Chippendale China Cabinet** adds a web frame, drawers, a frame base, and a pediment top. That covers the basic elements needed to build a cabinet of almost any size or style.

Then we get to special cases. The **Entertainment Center** shows you how to wire the inside of a cabinet for audio and video equipment and how to ventilate the enclosed space to prevent heat from building up. The **Built-In Bathroom Vanity** shows you how to construct cabinets that will be permanently installed in your home and how to make a laminated countertop. In the course of each project, you'll see how to adjust the size of a cabinet and how to alter the style to suit your own needs and tastes.

Now and then, I leave the story (briefly) to show you a *Quick Fixture* that will help speed up an operation or improve its accuracy. Or, to impart some useful *Shop Savvy* or *Methods of Work.* For example:

- The **router plane** makes it a snap to cut a hinge mortise to a precise, even depth.
- The **corner square** helps you glue up perfectly square cases and drawers.
- The **sawing grid** and the **circular saw guide** make it possible to cut large sheets of plywood easily and accurately in a small shop.
- A **dead man** helps you hang a cabinet on a wall without having to call one or two people over to hold it up while you drive the fasteners.

I also show you how to use wood grain to its best visual effect in a cabinet, how to make special joints, how to hang drawers and doors with a variety of hardware, how to fit and attach moldings, and how to apply plastic laminates.

Most important, in the little asides called *Oops!* and *No Problem,* you'll find out how to avoid some common cabinetmaking pitfalls and how to fix mistakes. No project is mistake-free; a good craftsman simply knows how to hide them. So I show you some useful secrets, such as how to reposition a door when the hinges are just a hair off the mark or how to square a cabinet case after you've assembled it.

And throughout, the *Look Here!* boxes help you navigate the book and find the information you need. For example, there's no sense in explaining how to true lumber to make a perfectly flat door or square drawer in each and every project, so I invite you to *Look Here!* in the one place in the book where I do explain it every time I feel that the knowledge might be helpful.

I've done it this way to make it easier for you to build the cabinet you want. You don't have to follow my play-by-play description of how to make a spice cupboard or an entertainment center; you can adjust the size, the style, or even mix and match elements. Add a glazed door and a face frame to the spice cupboard if it suits you. Or some crown molding and a frame base to the entertainment center to dress it up.

Cabinetmaking opens a world of possibilities; this book helps you take advantage of all of them.

With all good wishes,

Nick

Contents

Spice Cupboard

This is just about as simple a cabinet as you can build — a wooden box with a few shelves and a door. I asked Mary Jane Favorite, the furniture designer I work with, for a basic cabinet to begin this book, and she chose to recreate this eighteenth-century hanging cupboard. The design is proof, I think, that simple and elegant often go hand in hand.

Of course, elegant furniture designs go nowhere without thoughtful craftsmanship. The cupboard pictured is the work of Jim McCann, the master craftsman who is so often on the receiving end of Mary Jane's designs.

Jim, as you might expect, added his own touches. One of the best, I think, is the narrow strip that runs along the bottom of the cupboard, at the front — what I've called the *plinth* in the Materials List. It seems a simple thing, hardly worth a mention. But Mary Jane's original design didn't include it, as she intended the cabinet to be hung. By adding the plinth, Jim made it possible to rest the cabinet on a counter or table and use it freestanding. The plinth raises the bottom of the door a short distance and keeps it from rubbing the surface on which the cupboard rests. That one tiny part doubles the usefulness of the design. Craftsmanship is in the details.

What size should it be?

Where do you start when you set out to make a cabinet? You start with something to store. A cabinet is nothing more than a wooden container that encloses whatever it was designed to hold. How you make the cabinet depends a great deal on what you want to put in it.

The original eighteenth-century cupboard after which this one is patterned was sized to hold dried herbs stored in small containers. It could still serve the same function, although Jim tells me he plans to use it to store videotapes and compact discs. As it's designed, it will hold a variety of small and medium-size items.

When you're sizing a cabinet to store specific items, there are several rules of thumb you might want to keep in mind.

RULE 1 Whatever you store in the cabinet must be easy to retrieve. You should be able to see and reach the contents without having to search for what you want or move a lot of stuff.

Don't make the shelves so deep that things get buried toward the back. You may be able to store more stuff in a deeper cabinet, but will you ever find it again?

This hanging kitchen cupboard is built in much the same manner as the spice cupboard, but it's larger and deeper to accommodate plates, dishes, and kitchen appliances.

Our "tool shrine," as Jim and I call it, is sized to hold hand tools. We didn't want to make it too deep, or else every time we needed a tool, we'd have to move a dozen. But we wanted it to hold as many hand tools as possible. So we made the doors shallow boxes — this lets us store a lot of small tools inside the doors.

Space the shelves so that there's ample room between them. You shouldn't have to squeeze items between the shelves — this, too, makes them difficult to retrieve.

Also consider the level of the cabinet shelves. The highest shelf should be only as high as you can comfortably reach. If the shelves are designed to be reached from a standing position, this is between 72 and 78 inches above the floor for most people. If you plan to reach the shelves while sitting down — seated at a desk or counter, perhaps — the highest shelf should be no more than 58 to 60 inches above the floor. On floor-standing cabinets, the lowest shelf should be 3 to 4 inches above the floor for easy reach and to keep you from kicking whatever you've stored on there.

RULE 2 Don't make the cabinet so wide or the shelves so long that they sag. The "span" of the shelves should be short enough to support heavy objects without bowing under the burden.

How long should you make the shelves? That depends on the materials you're using and the weight of the objects you intend to store. Every woodworking material has a different "stiffness" rating, or *modulus of elasticity.* Consequently, some materials will hold more weight than others. Generally, solid wood is the best material for shelves; it sags less than plywood and particleboard.

What if the cabinet you want to build is wider than the acceptable span of the shelving material?

No problem — install one or more vertical *dividers* inside the cabinet. Dividers break up long spans so you can keep the shelves short.

TRY THIS!

If you are unsure whether the material you want to use will span a gap without sagging, perform a simple test. Make a single shelf from the material, cutting it a few inches longer than the span. Rest the shelf across two blocks, then weight it down with books or bricks to simulate the maximum load. Measure the height of the shelf above the workbench at each end and halfway in between — the difference is the amount of sag. If the shelf sags any more than $1/32$ inch per foot, reduce the span, use a different material, or reinforce the shelves.

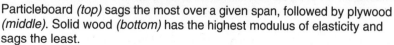

Particleboard *(top)* sags the most over a given span, followed by plywood *(middle).* Solid wood *(bottom)* has the highest modulus of elasticity and sags the least.

DIVIDER

If the shelving span is too long, add one or more dividers to your cabinet design. These vertical members partition the space inside the cabinet, reducing the distance that the shelves must span.

MAXIMUM SHELVING SPANS *(for 10-inch-wide shelving supporting 20 pounds per linear foot)*

MATERIAL	MAXIMUM SPAN	MATERIAL	MAXIMUM SPAN
¾"-thick Particleboard	24"	¾" Particleboard reinforced with a ¾" × 1½" oak strip glued edge to edge	28"
¾"-thick Plywood	30"	¾" Particleboard reinforced with two ¾" × ¾" oak strips glued to one face	34"
¾"-thick Yellow Pine	36"	¾" Particleboard reinforced with a ¾" × 1½" oak strip glued face to edge	34"
1"-thick Yellow Pine	48"	¾" Particleboard reinforced with two ¾" × 1½" oak strips glued face to edge	40"
1½"-thick Yellow Pine	66"	¾" Plywood reinforced with a ¾" × 1½" oak strip glued edge to edge	33"
¾"-thick Oak	48"	¾" Plywood reinforced with two ¾" × ¾" oak strips glued to one face	42"
1"-thick Oak	54"	¾" Plywood reinforced with a ¾" × 1½" oak strip glued face to edge	42"
1½"-thick Oak	78"	¾" Plywood reinforced with two ¾" × 1½" oak strips glued face to edge	48"

NO PROBLEM ■ *Correcting Sagging Shelves*

What do you do when the shelves in your cabinet sag and you can't change their span or the material from which they are made? No problem. There are several ways to solve this dilemma.

The standard wisdom is to turn the shelves over from time to time. I've even seen manufacturers of cheesy particleboard cabinets recommend this in their assembly instructions. But that can get to be a pain in the neck, and it doesn't really solve the problem. Here are three more permanent solutions:

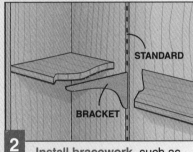

2 **Install bracework,** such as standards and brackets, at the back of the cabinet to help support the shelves in the middle of the span.

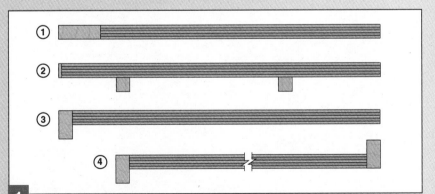

1 **Reinforce the shelves** to make them stronger. There are several ways to do this, listed from least to most effective. (1) Face the material with a solid strip of hardwood. (2) Attach strips of hardwood to the bottom face of the shelf. (3) Cover the front edge with a strip of hardwood glued face to edge. And finally, (4) the most effective method is to face *both* edges with hardwood strips glued face to edge. Arrange the back strip so it serves as a backstop.

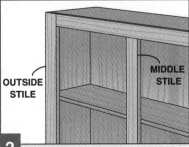

3 **Attach a vertical stile** to the front of the cabinet, between the two sides. If the shelves are fixed, attach them to this stile. If they are adjustable, install shelving supports to the inside face of the stile.

RULE 3 Make the cabinet a pleasing shape. This is not just a matter of taste. There are concrete guidelines for furniture proportions, and one of the most widely used is the *golden section*. Dating as far back as ancient Greece, architects and designers found they could better satisfy the public sense of proportion by dividing lines and shapes into sections so that when you divide the smaller part (a) by the larger part (b), you got the same result as when you divided the larger part by the whole (a + b):

$$a \div b = b \div (a + b)$$

The ratio that satisfies this condition is 1 to 1.618. When drawing a rectangular shape (such as the front of a cabinet), multiply the smaller dimension by 1.618 to find the larger one. Or divide the larger dimension by 1.618 to find the smaller. A rectangle in which the larger dimension is 1.618 times the smaller one is known as a *golden rectangle*.

Besides these three rules of thumb, there are other important considerations:

■ When sizing the doors, don't make them so wide that you have to step back to open them. If a door seems abnormally wide to you, divide it into two smaller doors.

■ If the cabinet is designed to hang on a wall, consider the combined weight of the cabinet and the stored items. Even a small cabinet can get quite heavy if you're using it to hold books, canned goods, or other heavy, dense things. A weighty cabinet should be attached to wall studs to help

TRY THIS!

You can construct a golden rectangle without multiplication, if you so wish. Start with the smaller dimension and draw a square. Place the point of a compass midway along one of the sides, and adjust it so the scribe touches an opposite corner. Swing an arc as shown, then extend the side where you placed the compass point through the arc. This will give you the larger dimension of the rectangle.

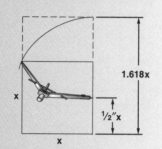

support the weight. Decide where you want to hang the cabinet, find the locations of the studs, and size your cabinet so it can be attached to one or more of the studs. You should also add a *nailing strip* at the back of the case, just under the top, to strengthen the case where it is attached to the wall.

■ Also consider the depth of the shelves in hanging cabinets. The deeper the shelves, the more stress a given weight exerts upon the structure as it hangs. Additionally, deep cabinets look ungainly when hung on a wall. For these reasons, hanging cabinets are seldom more than 15 inches deep.

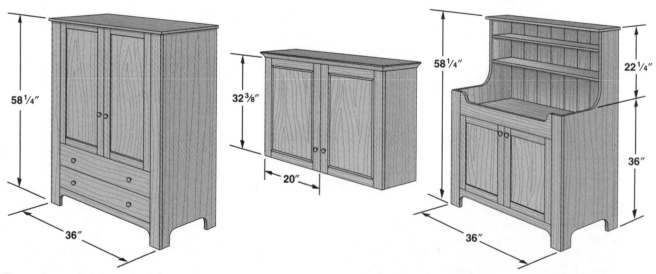

These three sketches of cabinets show various ways in which you might use a golden rectangle when designing furniture. The first, on the left, is the most obvious. The front profile is a golden rectangle. On the middle cabinet, the doors are golden rectangles. And on the right, not only is the overall front profile of the cabinet a golden rectangle, the profile of the top section is a golden rectangle laid on its side.

What style will it be?

As Mary Jane designed it, the spice cupboard is built in a "country" style. This is a simple, utilitarian style with classic elements. Old-time country cabinetmakers were inspired by eighteenth- and nineteenth-century "classic" styles — Queen Anne, Chippendale, Federal, and Empire — and they often had the skill to duplicate them. But their clients didn't have the wherewithal to pay for them. So the craftsmen made simpler "downscale" pieces.

If the country look doesn't suit your fancy, you can easily change the style without altering the basic construction of the cabinet.

UTILITARIAN STYLE

The simple, clean lines of these hanging shop cabinets are almost devoid of any style, but they are highly functional. Furniture designers call these sorts of pieces "utilitarian" — looks are unimportant; the design must be as useful as possible. This isn't to say that the piece can be ugly. Many elegant twentieth-century styles grew out of an emphasis on utility — "form follows function."

SOUTHWEST STYLE

In 1521, when the Spanish conquered New Spain — the area we know as Mexico, California, Arizona, and New Mexico — they found skilled woodworkers among the natives. As part of their missionary efforts, the Spanish taught the native craftsmen to build European furniture. The Spanish designs were a unique blend of European and African art forms. When the African Moors ruled Spain during medieval times, the Spanish adopted their design traditions, the *mujedar.* Native American woodworkers found the geometric patterns of the *mujedar* remarkably similar to their own, and the two decorative styles, Islamic and Indian, combined to create the unique Southwest style. This Southwest cabinet is ventilated due to the hot climate. It's decorated with intricately shaped slats and is brightly painted. On many Southwest cabinets, the backstop is moved to the front to simulate a bonnet or a pediment.

POSTMODERN STYLE

The Postmodern style combines elements of classic design with contemporary forms — a blend of old and new. This elegant Postmodern cabinet, built by Rick Goehring of Gambier, Ohio, has the clean, austere lines of a modern piece, but the moldings remind us of earlier pieces. This, and the spectacular tiger maple grain pattern, turn what might have been an ordinary cabinet into something quite extraordinary.

SHOP SAVVY ■ *Designing with Wood Grain*

As I said earlier in this book, craftsmanship is in the details. And one of the most commonly overlooked design details in woodworking is wood grain. The grain is a strong visual element that can either complement the project design or detract from it. Here are several tricks to help the wood grain complement your designs.

1 If the design is symmetrical, arrange the wood grain symmetrically. The cabinet on the left has two visually different door panels, each showing strikingly different grain patterns. As a result, the cabinet looks out of balance. The door panels in the cabinet on the right were book-matched — resawn from the same board and opened like a book so they are mirror images of each other. This reinforces the symmetry.

TRY THIS!

To get the best possible color match in wood, buy lumber all cut from the same tree. Small sawyers often provide this service for their customers, labeling or stacking their wood so you can easily match boards.

2 Match the wood grain in the narrow parts. Don't pay attention to just the broad expanses of wood; the grain in the narrow rails and stiles also has a visual impact. Random grain patterns *(left)* often muddy the design, and straight grain *(middle)* is visually uninteresting. By carefully choosing and matching the grain *(right),* you can create many pleasing effects.

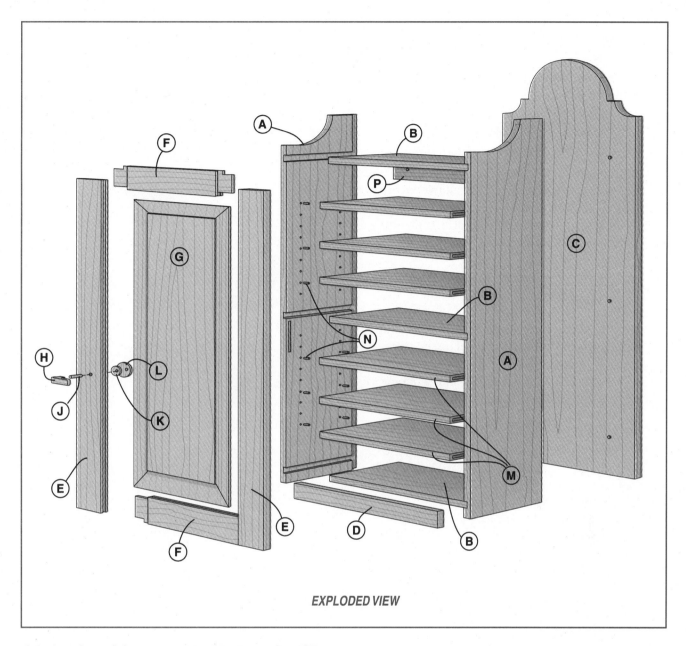

EXPLODED VIEW

SPICE CUPBOARD ■ *MATERIALS LIST*

PARTS

A	Sides	$5/8'' \times 7^{3}/8'' \times 36''$
B	Fixed shelves (3)	$5/8'' \times 6^{3}/4'' \times 13^{3}/8''$
C	Back	$5/8'' \times 13^{1}/4'' \times 41^{1}/2''$
D	Plinth	$5/8'' \times 1^{1}/2'' \times 14''$
E	Door stiles (2)	$5/8'' \times 2^{1}/2'' \times 30^{1}/2''$
F	Door rails (2)	$5/8'' \times 2^{1}/2'' \times 12''$
G	Door panel	$5/8'' \times 9^{3}/4'' \times 26^{3}/4''$
H	Turn pull	$5/8'' \times 5/8'' \times 1^{3}/4''$
J	Pivot dowel	$3/8''$ dia. $\times 1^{5}/8''$

K	Spacer	$1''$ dia. $\times 1/4''$
L	Latch disc	$1^{1}/2''$ dia. $\times 1/4''$
M	Adjustable shelves (1–6)	$5/8'' \times 6^{3}/4'' \times 12^{5}/8''$
N	Shelving support pins (4–24)	$1/4''$ dia. $\times 1''$
P	Nailing strip (optional)	$5/8'' \times 2^{1}/2'' \times 12^{3}/4''$

HARDWARE

#6 × 1½″ Flathead wood screws (6)

How do I build it?

Okay. We've determined the cabinet's size, proportion, and style. Now we can cut some wood.

PREPARING THE MATERIALS

Both Jim and I like to begin a project by "busting down" the lumber. That is, we true the lumber, plane it to the desired thickness, and cut all the parts to size. Before we bust down a board, we lay out the rough shapes of the parts on the surface, carefully choosing and matching wood grain.

TRY THIS!

Jim also labels *everything* — not only the parts, but the tops, bottoms, rights, lefts, insides, and outsides. Remember what I said about designing with wood grain on page 8? The labels help Jim to remember which board goes where and how to orient each for the best visual effect.

Jim chose curly cherry for this project because he wanted to make it a formal piece. Dark woods have a formal, classic look; lighter woods are more casual and contemporary. Cherry develops a rich, dark patina several months after you work it. The wood darkens as it ages, and it darkens more quickly when it's exposed to direct sunlight. As Mary Jane designed it, the spice cupboard requires about 12 board feet of 4/4 ("four-quarters") lumber, planed to ⅝ inch thick.

MAKING A CABINET CASE

A cabinet case is a box open on one side. At its simplest, it has just five parts — two sides, top, bottom, and back. As mentioned earlier, it may have additional parts, such as dividers or fixed shelves. This cabinet has a fixed middle shelf, adjustable shelves, a nailing strip, and a plinth at the bottom.

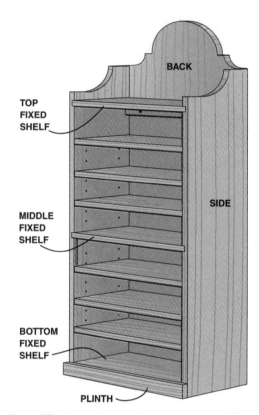

The "case" for the spice cupboard consists of those parts that are rigidly joined to form an enclosed space with an opening at the front.

Before you can "bust down" lumber, you must decide how you will cut the parts from each board, then lay out the parts on it. Remember to leave adequate room between the parts for saw kerfs.

After laying out the parts, label them. It's much easier to label the parts before you cut them than it is to try to identify them after they're cut.

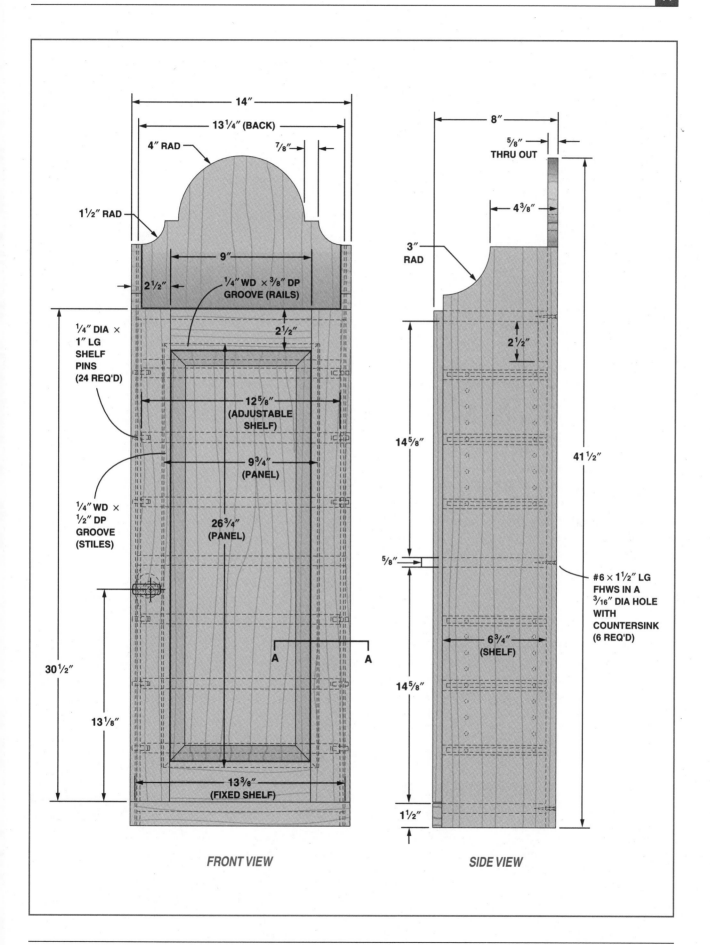

FRONT VIEW   SIDE VIEW

CUTTING THE JOINERY The spice cupboard case is joined with the simplest of joints — rabbets and dadoes cut in the sides, as shown in the *Left Side Layout* on page 14. This joinery is typical for cabinet cases, even large ones.

There are two common power tools used for making these joints — a router (either hand-held or mounted to a table) and a dado cutter mounted on a table saw. I prefer the dado cutter for most "through" joints — it's easy to set up and removes stock more quickly than a router. When correctly sharpened, a dado cutter leaves a surface almost as smooth as a good saw blade does.

A router, however, is the best tool for making stopped joints. If you use the tool hand-held, you can see the cut as it progresses and know when to stop. It also removes most of the waste from the stopped end. There's only a little cleanup work to do with a chisel, usually just to square the corners. A dado cutter, because it has a larger radius, leaves more waste — and more cleanup work to do.

Routing Case Joints. When routing dadoes and grooves, use a straight bit or a mortising bit to make the cuts. You can also use a straight bit to cut rabbets, but I like a piloted rabbeting bit. The pilot bearing on the end of the bit follows the edge of the wood and guides the bit.

When using a bit without a pilot, you must devise some way to guide the router. The guide need be nothing more than a straightedge clamped to the board you plan to cut. However, several years ago author/craftsman Bill Hylton showed me a great alternative. He makes disposable T-squares from scraps of wood or plywood. The crossbar automatically squares the straightedge to the edge of the board, eliminating a good deal of measuring. Jim improved on the design by adding a scrap of plywood underneath the straightedge to help align the jig.

COMMON CASE JOINERY

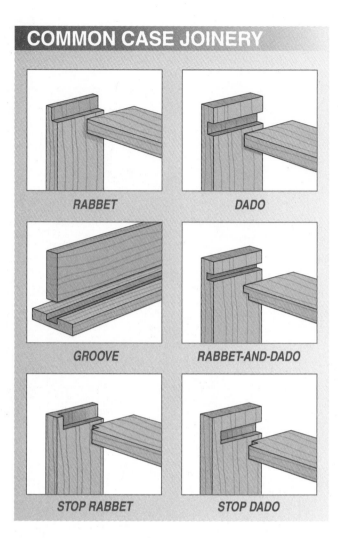

RABBET   DADO

GROOVE   RABBET-AND-DADO

STOP RABBET   STOP DADO

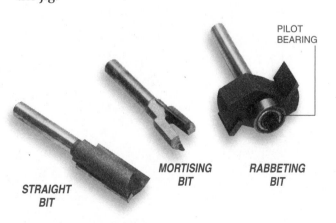

PILOT
BEARING

STRAIGHT
BIT

MORTISING
BIT

RABBETING
BIT

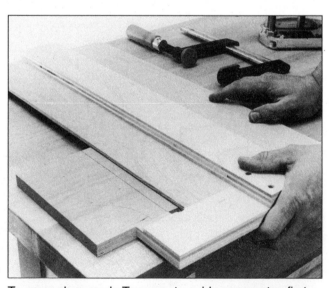

To use a shop-made T-square to guide your router, first lay out the joints on the case parts. Align the cut edge of the base with the layout lines, then clamp the straightedge to the board. Rout the joint, keeping the router firmly against the straightedge as you cut.

QUICK FIXTURES ■ *T-Square Router Guide, Router Edge Guide*

When using a hand-held router and an unpiloted bit to cut joinery, the most time-consuming part of the operation is positioning the guide on the work. The shop-made T-Square Router Guide simplifies that task. When you push the crossbar against the board, it aligns the straightedge perpendicular to the edge of the board. The replaceable base, once it's cut to size, helps you position the straightedge quickly.

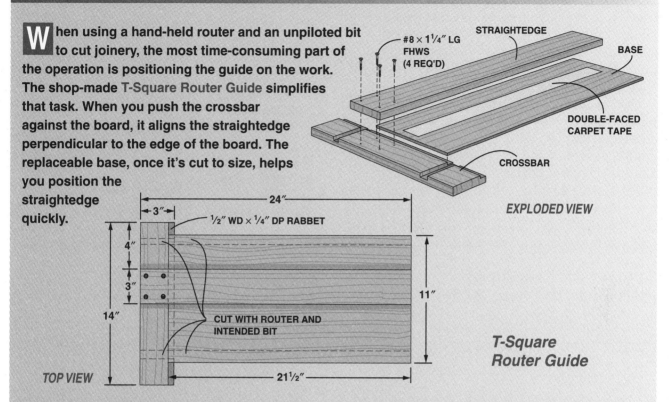

#8 × 1¼" LG FHWS (4 REQ'D)

STRAIGHTEDGE

BASE

DOUBLE-FACED CARPET TAPE

CROSSBAR

EXPLODED VIEW

24"

3"

½" WD × ¼" DP RABBET

4"

3"

14"

11"

CUT WITH ROUTER AND INTENDED BIT

21½"

TOP VIEW

T-Square Router Guide

When you're making long grooves and rabbets (such as the rabbets on the back edges of the spice cupboard sides), even a T-square guide can be difficult to set up. For these operations, Jim and I developed this Router Edge Guide that attaches to your router. It works in the same way as commercial edge guides, but there's one important difference: The fence is much longer. This makes it easier to control the router. Consequently, the cuts you make are more accurate.

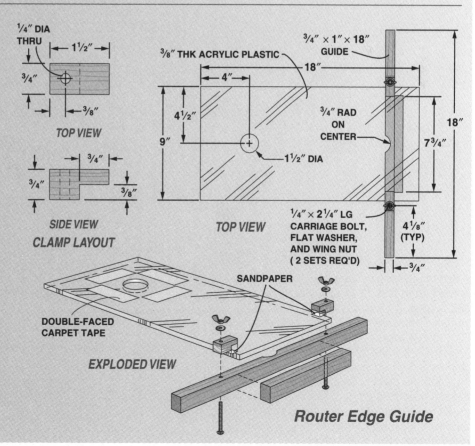

¼" DIA THRU

1½"

¾"

⅜"

TOP VIEW

¾"

¾"

¾"

⅜"

SIDE VIEW
CLAMP LAYOUT

⅜" THK ACRYLIC PLASTIC

4"

4½"

9"

1½" DIA

TOP VIEW

¾" × 1" × 18" GUIDE

18"

¾" RAD ON CENTER

18"

7¾"

¼" × 2¼" LG CARRIAGE BOLT, FLAT WASHER, AND WING NUT (2 SETS REQ'D)

4⅛" (TYP)

¾"

SANDPAPER

DOUBLE-FACED CARPET TAPE

EXPLODED VIEW

Router Edge Guide

You can also attach an edge guide directly to your router. Like a pilot, an edge guide follows the edge of a board, guiding the router bit as you cut rabbets and grooves. There are commercial edge guides available, but many of these are too small for really accurate work. Jim and I devised our own edge guide with a long fence.

Making Joints with a Dado Cutter. A dado cutter mounts to your table saw like a saw blade, but it cuts a much wider swath. To make a dado or a groove, pass the wood across the cutter, guiding it along the fence or pushing it with the miter gauge. When making a rabbet, attach a wooden face to the fence. Make a semicircular cutout in the face by slowly and carefully raising the dado blade into the face, using the depth-of-cut adjustment. This cutout accommodates the blade and lets you bring the fence right up against the dado cutter, or even position it over the cutter.

OOPS!

How can you combat a dado cutter's evil tendency to lift and tear the wood grain around the edges of the joint? Score the layout lines that mark the joint with a bench knife. This cuts the wood fibers near the surface so the dado teeth can't lift them. The top dado in this piece of plywood wasn't scored, while the bottom dado was. Look at how much cleaner the joint turned out when it was scored first.

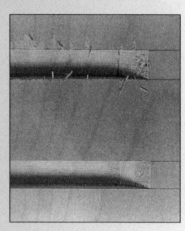

A dado cutter creates dadoes, grooves, and rabbets from ¼ to ¹³⁄₁₆ inch wide. A *stacked* dado cutter *(above)* is made up of two types of blades — outside *cutters* and inside *chippers*. Each blade is precisely ¼, ⅛, or ¹⁄₁₆ inch thick. To adjust the width of the cut, add or subtract chippers. For odd sizes, insert *dado shims* between the blades. These come in thicknesses from 0.004 to 0.031 inch. **Tip: You can make your own shims from paper, plastic laminate, or metal *shim stock* (available at most automotive parts stores).**

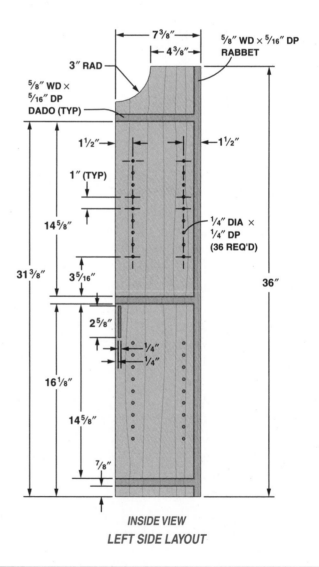

INSIDE VIEW
LEFT SIDE LAYOUT

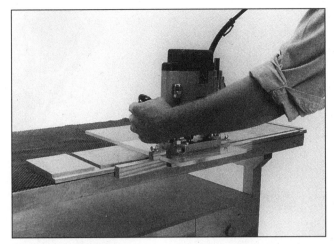

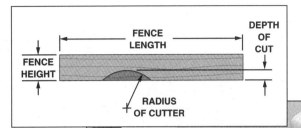

An edge guide is especially useful for cutting rabbets and grooves in long workpieces. Keep the fence of the guide firmly against the edge of the board as you rout.

When cutting dadoes and grooves, adjust the width of the cut by adding or subtracting chippers from the dado stack. Raise or lower the cutter to control the depth of cut.

To cut a rabbet, stack the cutter a little wider than the cut you want to make. Attach a wooden face with a semicircular cutout to the table saw fence, and position the fence so the cutout partially covers the cutter. Adjust the width of the rabbet by moving the fence left or right.

SHOP SAVVY ■ *Fitting Case Joints*

Because it's more difficult to add wood to a board than it is to cut it away, I've gotten in the habit of cutting on the "long side" of my layout line when making a joint. This often makes it necessary to trim a cut in order to get the joint to fit properly.

Several hand tools work wonders for this task.

■ I use a *rabbet plane* to shave the shoulders of a rabbet.

■ I trim the sides of dadoes and grooves with a *side rabbet plane*.

■ Finally, I clean out the bottom of dadoes and grooves with a shop-made *router plane*. You'll find the plans for this particular tool on page 25.

How tight should a joint fit? I always aim for a "slip fit." I don't want any slop in the joint, but I want to be able to assemble it without beating on the wooden parts.

RABBET PLANE

SIDE RABBET PLANE

ROUTER PLANE

MAKING ADJUSTABLE SHELVES Once Jim had cut the dadoes and rabbets in the sides, he drilled several rows of stopped holes. These holes hold the hardware that supports the adjustable shelves.

There are many types of adjustable shelving hardware, but they all boil down into three categories:

■ *Shelving support pins* are the easiest way to install adjustable shelving in a cabinet. The pins rest in holes spaced every 1 to 2 inches apart. They may be made from wood, metal, or plastic and come in many different styles.

■ *Wire supports* are mounted in rows of holes, much like pin supports. Stopped grooves cut in the ends of the shelves fit over the supports. These grooves are stopped at the front edges so you can't see the supports or the grooves when the shelves are installed.

■ *Standards and brackets* consist of slotted metal strips (the standards) that hold metal clips or brackets. The standards can be mounted directly to the inside surfaces of a cabinet, or you can recess them in grooves.

Shelving support pins come in all different styles, from utilitarian to decorative. Most are designed to support wooden shelves, although a few are made for glass. These pins usually fit in ¼-inch-diameter, ½-inch-deep holes, although a few European brands require 5-millimeter holes. You can also purchase metal sockets to line the holes. These make the pins easier to remove and replace, keep them from wearing the sides of the holes, and add decoration.

Wire supports fit into slots in the ends of the shelves and are completely hidden when the shelves are in place. They cannot work loose, and they keep the shelves from tipping.

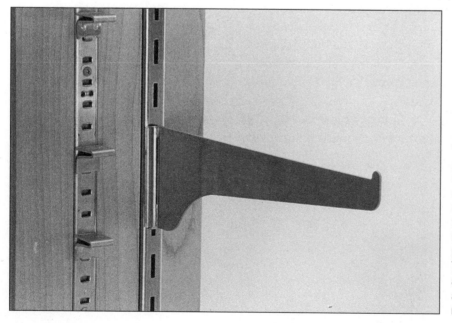

Side-mounted standards *(left)* have horizontal slots that mount small metal clips or brackets. Back-mounted standards *(right)* have vertical slots, and the brackets are as long as the shelves are wide. Side-mounted standards are less obtrusive and can be effectively hidden by recessing them in grooves. Back-mounted standards are more visible, but they are better if you must support a heavy load on the shelves. They can be mounted anywhere along the back of the cabinet case, allowing you to use as many as necessary.

Making Captured Pins. Jim decided to use wooden pins to support the shelves in the spice cupboard, mainly because we had a million of them on hand. However, Mary Jane didn't want the pins to show because this was supposed to be an old-time spice cupboard. So the two of them put their heads together and came up with a "captured pin" system. It works in much the same way as wire supports. The pins rest in rows of evenly spaced holes, and the ends of the shelves are cut with stopped grooves. When the shelves slide over the pins, the pins are "captured" in both the grooves and their holes and are hidden from sight.

The first step in making this system was to drill the holes for the pins. These had to be spaced evenly, every 1 inch on center. Additionally, all four rows had to be drilled precisely the same, or the grooves in the shelves wouldn't fit over the pins. To ensure accuracy, Jim developed a simple hole-spacing guide to position the drill as he made the holes.

TRY THIS!

If the hole-spacing guide will be used over and over again, install steel drill guides in the template. These metal bushings line the holes, preventing the drill bit from reaming out the wooden template and enlarging the holes.

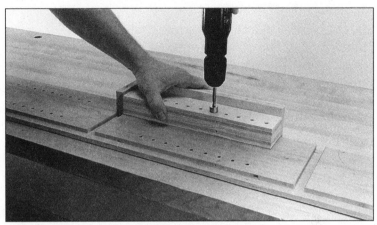

When you must make several rows of *matching holes,* it's best to make a template or *hole-spacing guide.* The guide shown is a double thickness of plywood with a row of evenly spaced holes to position and guide the drill bit. A cleat on the side positions the guide relative to the edge of the board. The cleat at the end positions it relative to a shelf dado or the end of the board.

QUICK FIXTURE ■ *Hole-Spacing Guide*

This jig positions shelving support holes and guides the drill bit as you bore them. It eliminates a lot of layout work and makes it easy to locate the holes accurately. The hole spacing on the jig is duplicated precisely every time you drill a set.

To make the jig, glue two long scraps of ¾-inch plywood together face to face. After the glue dries, trim the assembly to size, mark the holes where you want them, and drill the holes on a drill press. Then attach a cleat to one edge and one end. Note that the cleats overhang both the top and bottom faces of the guide. This lets you flip the jig over and align it with either the left or right edge of a board.

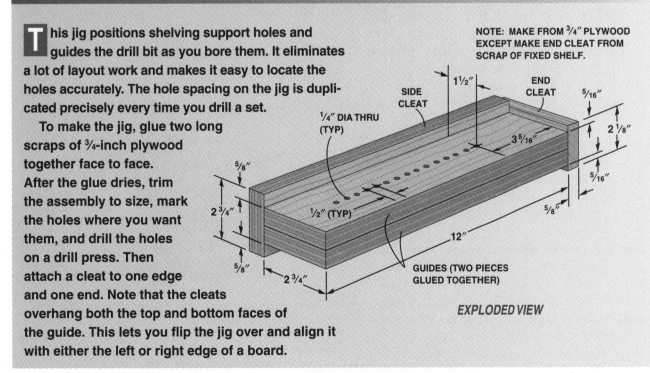

NOTE: MAKE FROM ¾" PLYWOOD EXCEPT MAKE END CLEAT FROM SCRAP OF FIXED SHELF.

SIDE CLEAT

END CLEAT

¼" DIA THRU (TYP)

1½"

3⁵⁄₁₆"

5⁄₁₆"

2⅛"

5⁄₁₆"

5⁄₈"

5⁄₈"

2¾"

½" (TYP)

12"

5⁄₈"

2¾"

GUIDES (TWO PIECES GLUED TOGETHER)

EXPLODED VIEW

After drilling the stopped holes in the sides, cut the profile of the sides (as shown in the *Side View* on page 11) and the profile of the back (as shown in the *Front View* on page 11). Also cut the stopped grooves in the edges of the adjustable shelves. As shown in the *Shelf Groove Detail–Top View* at right, these grooves have a radius on the stopped end. This is because Jim cut them with a dado cutter, and the blades left a curved surface where he halted the cut. The curve, however, serves no purpose. If you'd rather rout these grooves on a router table, go right ahead.

ASSEMBLING A CABINET CASE

Before gluing together a cabinet case — or *any* woodworking project, for that matter — perform a "dry" assembly. A dry assembly is a test assembly without glue, but you put the pieces together in the same order and use the same clamps to hold them together that you will for the glue-up. A dry assembly is a must for several reasons. It's your final check to make sure the joints fit properly. It helps you plan the glue-up procedure and set the clamps so you're not fumbling around when the glue is on the wood and its "working time" is ticking away. And, if you're assembling a large case, it lets you know if you need an extra pair of hands for the glue-up.

Assemble the sides and fixed shelves. However, do *not* attach the back with glue. The wood grain on the back is perpendicular to the shelves. If you glue it in place, the shelves will restrict its movement. Remember, wood expands and contracts across the grain with changes in relative humidity. If the back is glued in place, sooner or later it will either crack or push the cabinet apart.

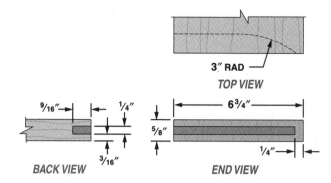

3" RAD

TOP VIEW

9/16"   1/4"   6 3/4"

5/8"

3/16"   1/4"

BACK VIEW   **END VIEW**

SHELF GROOVE DETAIL

Jim and I struggled with this problem when Mary Jane gave us the design for the cabinet. On most cabinet cases, the back is made from plywood. Because plywood is fairly stable, you don't have to worry about wood movement. But the back on this piece is solid wood. So Jim and I decided to attach the back with screws, driving them through holes that are slightly bigger than the screw shanks. This lets the back move slightly.

When cutting the grooves in the ends of the adjustable shelves, attach a tall fence to your table saw or router table fence. This will help keep the boards vertical, at the proper angle to the blade or cutter. Attach a stop to the tall fence to halt the cut short of the front edge.

NO PROBLEM ▪ *Squaring an Unsquare Case*

Y ou assemble the cabinet case, apply the clamps, check your assembly with a square, and...dagnabbit! The case went together cockeyed. Well, no problem. You can easily put it back to rights without taking it apart. The drawing sequence shows one option, the photos show two more.

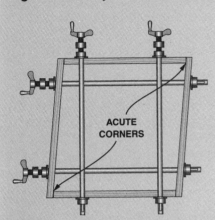

ACUTE CORNERS

1 One of the easiest tricks I've found for squaring up a large assembly is to simply shift the bar clamps that are holding it together. Check the corners of the assembly with a square, and identify the two acute (less than 90 degrees) corners.

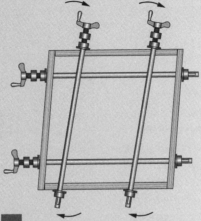

2 Loosen one or two of the clamps, and angle them slightly toward the acute corners.

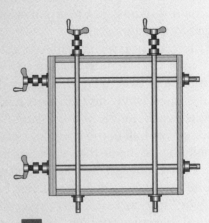

3 Slowly tighten the clamps, checking the corners with the square as you do so. The clamps will begin to pull the assembly back into alignment. When all the corners are square, stop tightening.

1/2" DIA
4"
2"
90°
45°

CORNER CAUL

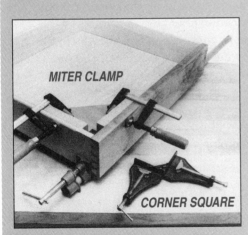

MITER CLAMP

CORNER SQUARE

When assembling small cases, use miter clamps or shop-made corner squares to help keep the corners at 90 degrees.

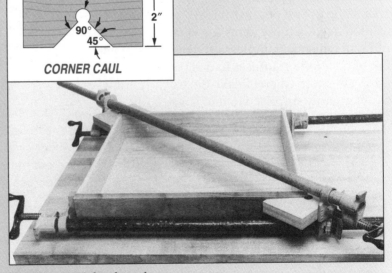

You can stretch a bar clamp diagonally from one acute corner to the other to pull an assembly square. Make a pair of these corner cauls to protect the corners.

Look Here! For more information on keeping assemblies square, see page 75.

MAKING A FRAME-AND-PANEL DOOR

There are several types of doors you might put on a cabinet. The easiest to make is a *slab* door — a single piece of plywood or particleboard, its edges covered with veneer or laminate. These, however, are most commonly used on contemporary and utilitarian furniture. Mary Jane chose a traditional *frame-and-panel* door to give the spice cupboard a more formal appearance.

There are also several different ways in which you might fit a door to a cabinet. *Overlaid* doors completely cover the front edges of the case. Sometimes, where double doors meet over a divider, each door is *half-overlaid.* That is, each door covers half of the front edge of the divider. Doors that fit inside the case are *inset.* Finally, you can cut a rabbet all the way around a door so the rabbets fit inside the door opening but the shoulders or "lips" cover it. These doors are *lipped.* The door of the spice cupboard is an overlaid frame-and-panel door.

Frame Joinery. Although there are many ways to join the parts of a frame-and-panel door, I prefer a haunched mortise-and-tenon joint. The major advantage of this joint, besides its strength, is that it incorporates a groove around the interior of the frame to hold the panel.

Don't be put off because it looks complex. I avoided making these joints for a good long while, under the mistaken impression that any joint with that many mating surfaces had to be a bother to make. However, when I finally did try the joint, I was pleasantly surprised to find it was fairly straightforward to cut. I use it often now.

FITTING A DOOR

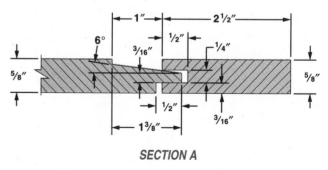

OVERLAY   HALF-OVERLAY

INSET   LIPPED

SHOP SAVVY

When building a frame-and-panel door, always make the panel slightly narrower across the grain than the space allowed for it. For example, on this cabinet, the space between the stiles is 9 inches, and the grooves are ½ inch deep, making the space allowed for the panel 10 inches. But Jim made the panel 9¾ inches wide. This gives the panel some room to expand and contract when the weather changes.

How much room should you allow? That depends on the width of the panel. The rule of thumb is to allow ¼ inch for every 12 inches across the grain on *plain-sawn* wood and ⅛ inch for every 12 inches of *quarter-sawn.* Remember, quarter-sawn wood moves only half as much across the grain as plain-sawn.

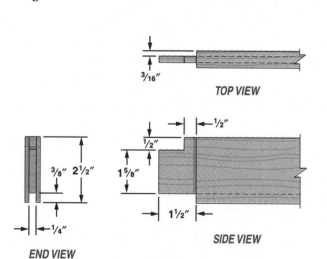

TOP VIEW

END VIEW

TENON LAYOUT

SIDE VIEW

SECTION A

METHODS OF WORK ■ *Making a Haunched Mortise-and-Tenon*

The haunched mortise-and-tenon joint was designed specifically for frame-and-panel doors. The grooves in the inside edges of the frame members hold the panel, the mortises and tenons join the members, and the *haunches* in the tenons fill the grooves at the very ends of the stiles.

1   **Begin by cutting the grooves** in the inside edges of the frame members with a dado cutter or a table-mounted router. The grooves must be centered in the edges. To make sure they are, I pass each piece over the cutter *twice,* once with each face of the piece against the fence. This ensures that the sides of the grooves are the same distance from each face.

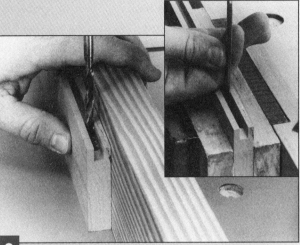

2   **Cut the mortises** near the ends of the stiles, either by drilling them out on a drill press or by routing them on a router table. If you use the drill press, first drill holes at the beginning and end of each mortise, then go back and drill overlapping holes between them. Clean up the sides and square the corners of the mortise with a chisel.

3   **Cut the tenons** in the ends of the rails. Begin by making the step or haunch on the table saw, cutting the *outside* edge of the board. Then cut the shoulder on the two faces. You don't need to cut the inside edge.

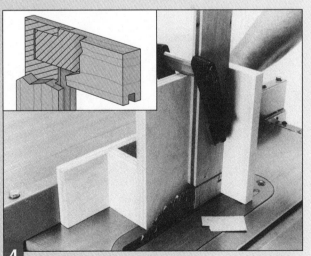

4   **Using a tenoning jig** (see page 22) to hold the rails vertically, cut the cheeks of the tenon. Finally, cut the outside edge of the tenon, completing the haunch.

Look Here! For more information on making haunched mortises and tenons, see page 120.

QUICK FIXTURE ■ *Tenoning Jig*

A tenoning jig is a carriage that holds boards vertically on a work surface. This lets you to make cuts in the *ends* of boards safely and accurately. It's especially useful for routing or cutting long, narrow boards — ones that are too narrow to be supported safely or accurately by a fence.

Assemble the jig from scraps of wood and plywood, joining the tall side, long side, and ends with glue and screws. Attach the backstop with *screws only*. This allows you to move the backstop right or left, turn it upside down, or replace it when it becomes chewed up. This way you can always have a fresh surface to back up a cut and prevent tear-out. It also allows you to adjust the width of the backup surface.

Jim and I designed this jig to ride along a fence or a straightedge. The long side gives you a lot of "guiding" surface and helps keep the work properly aligned with the cutter. Clamp the work to the tall side, with the back edge resting against the backstop. Adjust the position of the cut in the work by moving the fence right or left.

Important! Both the tall side and the backstop must be square to the worktable for this jig to work properly. If it isn't, you must sand the bottom edges until the jig rests square. Or, shim them with pieces of masking tape.

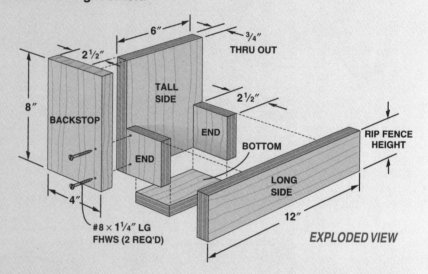

EXPLODED VIEW

The advantage to being able to change the width of the backstop is that you can mount the work with either the edge or the face against it. This lets you "cut around" the work to saw all four surfaces of a tenon.

If you need to hold the work at an angle to the blade, cut an angled backstop and screw it to the tall side. Remember to position the screws high enough so you won't nick them with a cutter. For added safety, use soft brass screws.

RAISING A PANEL The door to the spice cupboard has a raised panel. A raised panel has beveled or tapered ends and edges. (Old-timers say it's "thinned out" around the perimeter.) The flat area in the middle is called the *field,* and it's sometimes separated from the bevel by a *step.*

To make a raised panel, you must either cut a bevel all around the perimeter of the board or create a shape with a router or shaper. Before you can do either, however, you must decide how thin to make the panel at the ends and edges and, if you're sawing a bevel, what angle to make it. If you make the panel too thick at the edges or the bevel too steep, it will split the sides of the groove that holds it. A proper panel should just touch the groove's sides when it bottoms out in the groove.

Also decide whether the panel will have a step between the thinned-out portion and the field. Most craftsmen prefer to make a $\frac{1}{16}$- to $\frac{1}{8}$-inch step to help delineate the field. This makes the visual effect of the raised panel more dramatic.

There are two tools that I like to use to raise panels: a table-mounted router and a table saw. Each has its unique advantages.

Raising a Panel with a Router. When using a router and a panel-raising bit to create a panel, you have a choice of shapes you can make around the perimeter — bevel, cove, or ogee. (An *ogee* is an S-curve.) The bit cuts the portion of the panel that fits in the grooves so it is square to the ends and edges. Adjust the depth of cut so this part of the panel is as thick as the grooves are wide.

SAFEGUARD

Invest in *vertical panel-raising bits* if you plan to use your router to make raised panels. Avoid horizontal wing cutters. Because these have such a large radius, the tip speed can be very high, even if you reduce the router speed. This increases the risk of a dangerous kickback.

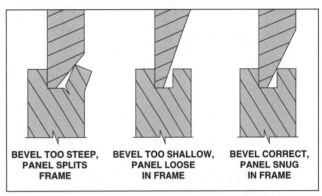

BEVEL TOO STEEP, PANEL SPLITS FRAME	BEVEL TOO SHALLOW, PANEL LOOSE IN FRAME	BEVEL CORRECT, PANEL SNUG IN FRAME

When sawing a raised panel with beveled edges, the bevel angle is critical. If it's too steep *(left),* the panel could split the frame that it's mounted in. If it's too shallow *(middle),* the panel will be too loose — it will rattle every time you open or close the door. The bevel should be angled so it barely touches the groove's side when the edge of the panel rests on the groove's bottom *(right).*

Strange to say, vertical panel-raising bits are best used *horizontally.* In this configuration, gravity works for you, making it easier to hold and feed the work. Mount your router in a joint maker (see page 114) or a similar horizontal routing jig. Pass the panel over the bit, cutting against the rotation. Rout the end of the panel first, then the edges. That way, if there is any tear-out when you cut across the grain, you'll remove it when you cut with the grain. For the smoothest possible surface, cut no more than $\frac{1}{8}$ inch deep with each pass. **Tip: If you must use the bit vertically in a router table, attach a *tall fence* (see page 24) to the regular fence to provide additional support for the wide panels.**

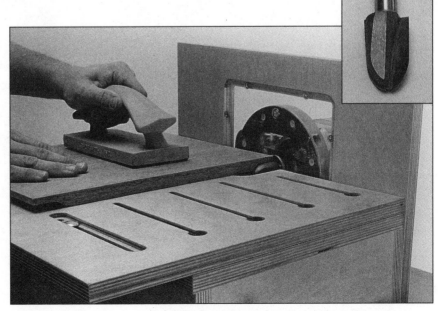

Raising a Panel with a Table Saw. The disadvantage of using a router to make a raised panel is that you can't change the slope of the taper. This limits the thickness of the stock you can use for the panel. A table saw will cut only a single shape — a straight bevel — but you can adjust the angle of the taper for any stock thickness.

Select a hollow-ground planer blade or a carbide-tipped ripping blade to make as smooth a cut as possible. Position the fence on the saw so you can tilt the blade *away* from it — this will reduce the risk of kickback and will prevent the saw teeth from biting into the fence. Attach a *tall fence* to the table saw fence to help support the panel as you make the cuts.

> **Look Here!** You can also make raised panels on a joint maker jig. For instructions on how to make this jig, see page 114.

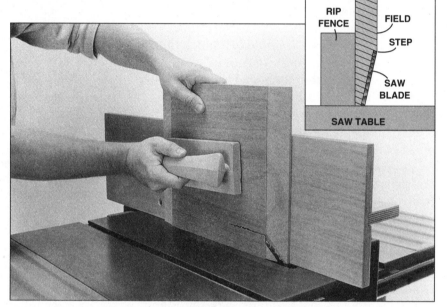

Cut the ends of the raised panel first, then the edges. If you want to make a step, carefully position the fence so just the outside corners of the saw teeth break through the wood as you cut. The tops of the teeth will create the step. To make the step smaller, move the rip fence away from the blade. To make it larger, move the fence closer. If you make the step wider than the teeth of the saw, you will have to make a second series of cuts around the perimeter of the field, cutting just deep enough to meet the bevel.

QUICK FIXTURE ■ *Tall Fence*

A tall fence extends an ordinary fence vertically. The large surface supports a wide board on its edge or end as you cut it.

The jig must be perfectly straight and flat to guide the work accurately. To make sure that our fence was as true as possible, Jim clamped the face to the work surface of our table saw as he glued the brace to it.

Once you've assembled the parts, attach the tall fence to the regular fence with bolts or screws. Countersink the heads so the hardware won't interfere with the work.

Check that the face of the tall fence is square to the work surface. If not, shim the tall fence with bits of masking tape above or below the mounting hardware until it rests at the proper angle.

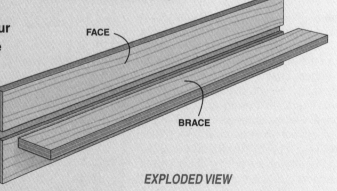

EXPLODED VIEW

ASSEMBLING THE DOOR The parts of the doors — rails, stiles, and panel — have to go together all at once. As you did when assembling the case, do a *dry assembly* first to check the fit of the parts and set the clamps. Then assemble the rails and stiles with glue. As you put them together, slide the panel in place in its grooves. However, do *not* glue the panel in the grooves. The panel should "float," free to expand and contract with changes in the weather.

SHOP SAVVY

Apply a finish to the panel and the inside surfaces of the grooves that hold it before you assemble a door. Otherwise, you might see unfinished surfaces when the panel shrinks during dry weather.

HANGING THE DOOR

To hang the door on the case, first fit it to its opening. Using a hand plane or scraper, carefully shave the door's edges until it fits the case properly.

SHOP SAVVY

Most craftsmen I know prefer to make the doors slightly large so they'll have a little to shave away when they fit the door. (It's much harder to stretch a door to fit an opening.) When making a lipped or an overlay door, make it about 1/16 inch taller and wider than what you figure you'll need. When making an inset door, make it the same size as the opening, then remove a little stock from the edges of the rails and stiles so it fits its opening with a 1/32- to 1/16-inch gap.

The spice cupboard door hangs on common butt hinges. These have to be *mortised* into the door frame and the case. That is, you must cut recesses for the hinge leaves. When the hinges are installed and the door is closed, all you should see of the hinges are the barrels, where the leaves are joined. Each leaf should be flush with the surface of the wood, although the less expensive varieties of butt hinges require that you set the leaves slightly below the surface.

QUICK FIXTURE ▪ *Router Plane*

A router plane is an invaluable aid for fitting joints and installing hardware. The L-shaped plane iron reaches down below the sole of the plane and cleans out the bottoms of dadoes, grooves, and mortises.

There are several commercial router planes available, but I prefer this shop-made version. Jim made it with a clear acrylic plastic base to help you see what you're cutting.

To use the router plane, loosen the thumbscrew and move the plane iron up or down to get the depth of cut you want. It's best not to try to remove more than 1/32 inch at a time. I've also found that it helps to swing the plane in an arc as you cut. Hold one end of the handle stationary and rotate the other end around it.

RESOURCES

Purchase the plane iron from:
**Garrett Wade
161 Avenue of the
Americas
New York, NY 10013**

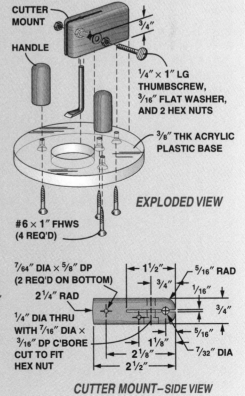

CUTTER MOUNT

HANDLE

1/4" × 1" LG THUMBSCREW, 3/16" FLAT WASHER, AND 2 HEX NUTS

3/8" THK ACRYLIC PLASTIC BASE

3/4"

EXPLODED VIEW

#6 × 1" FHWS (4 REQ'D)

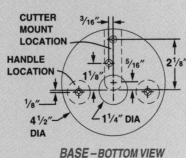

CUTTER MOUNT LOCATION

HANDLE LOCATION

3/16"

5/16"

1 1/8"

2 1/8"

1/8"

4 1/2" DIA

1 1/4" DIA

BASE – BOTTOM VIEW

7/64" DIA × 5/8" DP (2 REQ'D ON BOTTOM)

2 1/4" RAD

1/4" DIA THRU WITH 7/16" DIA × 3/16" DP C'BORE CUT TO FIT HEX NUT

1 1/2"

3/4"

5/16" RAD

1/16"

3/4"

5/16"

1 1/8"

2 1/8"

7/32" DIA

2 1/2"

CUTTER MOUNT – SIDE VIEW

The secret to setting butt hinges accurately is careful layout. You must precisely mark the positions of the hinges on the door frame and the case, then drill the pilot holes for the hinge screws dead center in the holes in the leaves. I use three tricks to maintain precision.

■ First of all, I mark the location of hinge mortises on the door and wedge the door in the case right where I want it. Then I transfer the marks on the door frame to the case, using a square to make sure both sets of marks are perfectly aligned.

■ When marking the outline of the leaves, I fold the hinge over the outside arris of the part so one leaf rests on the edge of the wood and the other against the face. (An arris, by the way, is where two surfaces come together. It's often confused with a corner, which is the junction of three surfaces.) By doing this, I'm using one leaf as a stop to position the other and all the leaves end up exactly the same distance in from the arris.

■ Finally, I use a self-centering bit like a "Vix" to drill the pilot holes. This ingenious little tool automatically centers the pilot holes in the hinge leaf holes.

METHODS OF WORK ■ *Setting a Mortised Hinge*

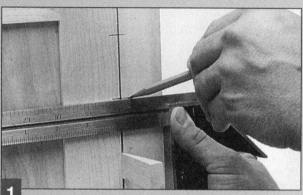

1 **To set a butt hinge,** first fit the door to the case, and either secure it with clamps or wedge it inside the opening so it's right where you want it. Using a square, mark the location of the hinge across both the door frame and the case.

2 **Remove the door** from the case, and cut the outlines of the hinge leaves where you have marked the assemblies. I like to hold the hinge in place with a bit of double-faced carpet tape while I trace around the perimeter with a pencil or a bench knife. I also fold the leaves over the arrises to position them all the same.

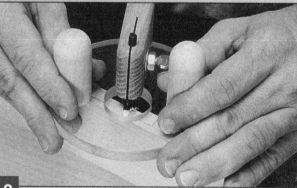

3 **Remove most of the waste** with a chisel without trying to get the bottom of the mortise perfectly flat. Then set a router plane to cut to a depth equal to the thickness of a hinge leaf. Use this to clean out the bottom of the mortise. The bottom will be perfectly flat and precisely the right depth.

4 **Rest the hinge** in its mortise, once again sticking it in place with carpet tape. Drill the pilot holes for the screws with a Vix bit, as shown. Finally, screw the hinge to the door and the case. Note: It's not absolutely necessary to stick the hinges down a second time, but I've found it helps prevent them from shifting when you drill the pilot holes.

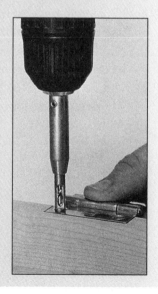

NO PROBLEM ■ *Repositioning a Door*

O kay, you set the hinges just like I showed you, you swing the door closed, and...it doesn't fit. No problem.

A cockeyed door, whether inset or overlay, is usually caused by misplacing a hinge. Setting a hinge just a small distance off the mark is often enough to cause the door to rub the case or even to prevent it from closing. But all you have to do to set things right is move the offending hinge just a little.

Swing the door open and shut a few times so you're sure where it's hitting or rubbing. Then take a look at the hinges. Are there any that look out of place? Were there any screw holes that were not perfectly aligned with the holes in the hinge leaves? If so, can you remember which ones?

Make your best guess as to which hinge leaf has to be moved, and remove the screws. Then shift the door slightly (while the other hinge is still attached) to see if you can get the door to fit properly. When you know what hinge needs to be moved and how much, remove the door.

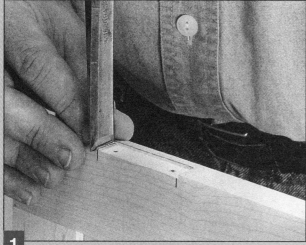

1 Depending on which direction you need to move the hinge, you may have to enlarge the mortise. Cut away the edge with a chisel, and clean out the bottom with a router plane. Don't worry that the mortise will now be slightly larger than the hinge. Usually, you have to move a hinge such a short distance that it's hardly noticeable.

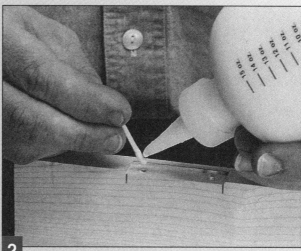

2 Plug the old screw holes with toothpicks and glue. Allow the glue to dry, and shave the toothpicks flush with the bottom of the hinge mortise. Then put the hinge in its new position and drill new pilot holes. **Tip: Use fast-setting epoxy glue. Not only does it set up faster, it fills the holes better.**

3 In extreme cases, you may have to drill out the screw holes and plug them with dowels. Or you may need to cut a block of wood and fill the mortise. The plugs in the screw holes will never show, but you must carefully match the grain and color of the wood when filling a mortise. If you do it right, the patch will be almost invisible, as shown in the smaller photo.

INSTALLING A DOOR LATCH Once the door is hung, you must have some way of opening it and keeping it closed.

Pulls, Catches, and Latches. There are any number of devices used to open and close a door, but they all fall into three categories. You may employ a two-part solution, using a *pull* to open the door and a *catch* to hold it closed. Or you can opt for a *latch,* a mechanism that opens the door and keeps it closed.

In keeping with the country style, Jim elected to make a *turn latch.* Hardware was a much more precious commodity in days gone by, and country craftsmen conserved it when possible. A turn latch requires no metal parts — it's a wooden knob or handle on the outside of the cabinet that turns a wooden latch or bar on the inside.

Making a Turn Latch. The turn latch that Jim designed for this project is unique. There were no interior parts that a latch could be made to catch on. So Jim cut a semicircular groove in the side of the cabinet and arranged a disc or *cam* to rest in the groove when the handle is turned counterclockwise.

To duplicate Jim's latch, first remember to cut the groove in the side *before* you assemble the case. Jim cut the groove with a dado cutter. He lowered the cutter beneath the work surface, clamped the side face down on the saw, then slowly raised the cutter. You could also use a biscuit joiner. Or, rout the groove — the bottom doesn't have to be curved.

Drill the latch hole in the door stile making it slightly larger than the dowel that joins the handle to the disc — about $7/16$ inch in diameter.

ALTERNATIVES ▪ *Door Hardware*

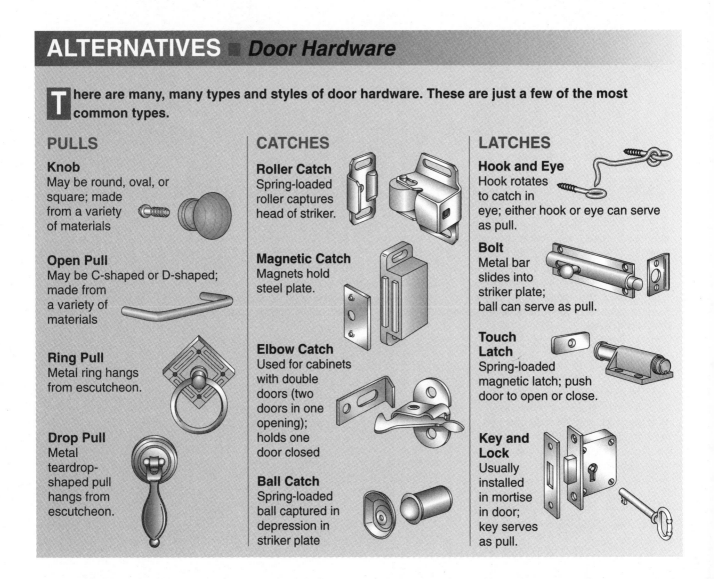

There are many, many types and styles of door hardware. These are just a few of the most common types.

PULLS

Knob
May be round, oval, or square; made from a variety of materials

Open Pull
May be C-shaped or D-shaped; made from a variety of materials

Ring Pull
Metal ring hangs from escutcheon.

Drop Pull
Metal teardrop-shaped pull hangs from escutcheon.

CATCHES

Roller Catch
Spring-loaded roller captures head of striker.

Magnetic Catch
Magnets hold steel plate.

Elbow Catch
Used for cabinets with double doors (two doors in one opening); holds one door closed

Ball Catch
Spring-loaded ball captured in depression in striker plate

LATCHES

Hook and Eye
Hook rotates to catch in eye; either hook or eye can serve as pull.

Bolt
Metal bar slides into striker plate; ball can serve as pull.

Touch Latch
Spring-loaded magnetic latch; push door to open or close.

Key and Lock
Usually installed in mortise in door; key serves as pull.

Cut the profiles of the handle, spacer, and disc on a band saw, then drill ⅜-inch-diameter holes in all three parts. Round the edges of the handle with a rasp or a file so it fits your hand comfortably.

Glue the dowel in the latch disc and let it dry. Sand the end of the dowel flush with the surface of the disc and slip the spacer over the dowel. Insert the dowel in the hole in the door stile from the *inside*. Glue the handle to the protruding end of the dowel. Position the handle so it's horizontal when the disc is resting in the groove in the side. As you do this, be careful not to get any glue on the door frame. You don't want the pieces of the latch to stick to it.

FINISHING THE SPICE CUPBOARD

Finishing is a highly individual matter; I've known craftsmen who believed more strongly in their own personal finishing procedures than they did their religion. But for those of you who aren't quite so set in your ways, I'll tell you how we finished this particular piece.

Applying Shellac. A formal cabinet such as this probably would have been finished with shellac. Jim and I chose an orange shellac to help darken the wood. We thinned the shellac to a "2-pound cut." This means 2 pounds of solid shellac to every gallon of alcohol solvent, although we didn't make nearly that much. Two ounces of shellac flakes in a cup of alcohol is equivalent to a 2-pound cut. The shellac you buy ready-mixed is usually a 3-pound cut; if you mix it 2 to 1 with alcohol, you'll get a 2-pound cut. The thinner cut brushes on in a thinner coat with fewer dimples and lap marks. This, in turn, makes it easier to sand between coats.

Actually, I sanded between every other coat, applying six coats in all. That sounds like a lot, but the shellac dries very quickly. You can easily build up that many coats in two days. After the final coat, wait for the shellac to harden for two days before rubbing it out with 600-grit wet/dry sandpaper, followed by an ultrafine abrasive such as pumice or rottenstone.

TRY THIS!

If you work with figured woods, such as the curly cherry used to make this spice cupboard, you can enhance the figure with a "wash coat" of aniline dye. Dilute full-strength dye 8 to 1 with distilled water, and brush it on the wood. Figured wood presents both end grain and long grain at the surface. More dye soaks into the end grain than long grain, emphasizing the difference between the two.

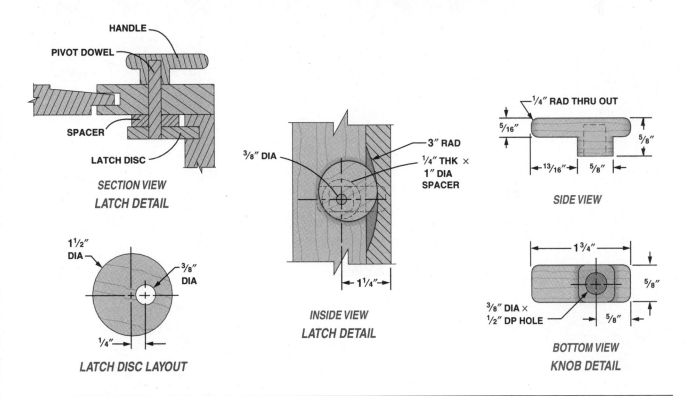

SECTION VIEW
LATCH DETAIL

LATCH DISC LAYOUT

INSIDE VIEW
LATCH DETAIL

SIDE VIEW

BOTTOM VIEW
KNOB DETAIL

Mission Bookcase

Although this piece is much larger than the spice cupboard, its construction is very similar. Both are cases filled with adjustable shelves. There are, however, several differences worth mentioning. The bookcase has a *face frame* to help strengthen the cabinet and enclose the front. The doors are glazed — that is, they have wooden frames with glass panels. And this piece can be made as a movable stand-alone unit *or a permanent built-in.*

The bookcase shown is built-in — it's one of several units. The units are fastened together and to the wall against which they sit. Making this bookcase so you can build it in is a simple matter of including a *nailing strip* along the back. This gives you something to attach the case to the wall. We'll go into this in more detail on page 48.

By the way, the bookcase (and the units it is attached to) was designed by Mary Jane Favorite and built on-site by a talented young cabinet-maker, Chris Walendzak.

What size should it be?

That, of course, depends on what you want to store in the case. This sort of cabinet is not just for storage; it's designed to protect and *display* its contents. The enclosed shelves in this bookcase protect my books from dust, but the glazed doors let me see the titles on the spines — I can search my library without having to open the cases. Curio cabinets, display cases, even cases for hunting and sporting equipment are made in a similar manner. The size and shape are always dictated by the objects that are displayed in the cabinet — and how many of them you have to display.

TRY THIS!

When displaying collectibles in a cabinet, make the shelves from thick, tempered glass. You may also want to mount a mirror in the back of the cabinet. This lets you see the objects from all sides.

This trapezoid-shaped curio cabinet was built to display collectibles. Both the doors and the sides are wooden frames with glass panels. This, combined with the angled sides, makes it easy to see the contents of the cabinet.

This is an interesting variation on a bookcase. These stacking cases are small boxes, each with its own glazed door. This system lets you expand your shelving space as your library grows. Note that the doors fold up and slide into their cases.

SHELF ARRANGEMENT

In addition to deciding on the overall size of the bookcase or display case, you must also arrange the shelves. To a large extent, the spacing between the shelves will be determined by the height of the objects you have to keep on them. But this is not the only factor.

MATHEMATICAL PROGRESSIONS Repetitive elements in an architectural design — like the shelves in a bookcase — look better if they are arranged according to a mathematical progression. A shelving unit in which the shelves are spaced precisely the same looks top-heavy. A better arrangement would be to follow a simple *arithmetic progression*. As you go down the case, the space between each set of shelves is a constant amount greater than the space above it. The largest space is at the bottom; the smallest, at the top. This makes the piece look more stable.

Arithmetic progression is only one of several possible systems you might use.

■ *Geometric progression* builds on a constant ratio. The series 8, 10, 12½, 15⅝ builds on a ratio of 1¼. Each number is 1¼ times the preceding number.

■ In a *harmonic progression*, the ratios are reciprocals of a sequence. You obtain a reciprocal by dividing a number into 1. The sequence 1/4, 1/5,

1/6, 1/7 is the harmonic of the sequence 4, 5, 6, 7. Multiply the harmonic sequence times a constant number, say 60, and you arrive at a shelf spacing of 15, 12, 10, and 8½.

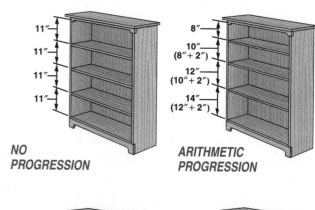

NO PROGRESSION   ARITHMETIC PROGRESSION

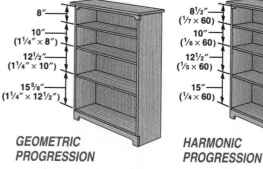

GEOMETRIC PROGRESSION   HARMONIC PROGRESSION

STANDARD BOOKCASE AND DISPLAY CASE SIZES

Standing Bookcase
Height: 30″–84″
Width: Depends on shelving span
Depth: 10″–12″
(Standard depth is 11½″)
Shelf spacing:
   Paperbacks 7″–8″
   Hardcover books 10″–12″
   Oversized books 13″–15″

Standing Display Cabinet
(Dolls, trophies, etc.)
Height: 30″–84″
Width: Depends on shelving span
Depth: 10″–18″
Shelf spacing: Depends on items displayed

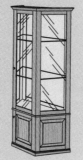

Hanging Display Cabinet
(Miniatures, small boxes, bells)
Height: 30″–42″
Width: Depends on shelving span
Depth: 3″–15″
Shelf spacing: Depends on items displayed

Fishing/Hunting Cabinet
(Rods, firearms, archery equipment)
Height: 60″–84″
Width: Depends on shelving span
Depth: 15″–24″
Shelf spacing: Depends on items displayed. Often, items are arranged in horizontal or vertical *racks*. Gun cabinets require locks.

What style will it be?

The bookcase shown in this chapter is made in a mission style. Mission, or *Arts and Crafts,* moved away from the ornate Victorian styles to a simpler one derived from old medieval and Gothic forms. Since my house was built in 1895 — the beginning of the Arts and Crafts movement in America — my wife and I thought it might be nice to outfit our library with bookcases from that era. However, there are dozens of other styles you might choose from. Here are three possibilities.

Courtesy of The Hermitage: Home of President Andrew Jackson, Nashville, TN

CLASSIC FEDERAL STYLE

Case pieces made in the Federal style (1780–1820) are light and graceful, often decorated with veneers and exotic woods. They often show molded shapes at the top, waist, and base. The glazed doors from this period were divided into many panes, usually multiples of 3. (Large panes were almost nonexistent.)

VICTORIAN OAK STYLE

Furniture from the late nineteenth century was often made of white oak and oak plywood. These pieces often showed contoured pediments, delicately curved legs, highly decorative hardware, and carved appliqués. Many pieces, such as this combination desk and bookcase, were asymmetrical.

CONTEMPORARY STYLE

Contemporary (1950–present) bookcases tend to be austere and rectilinear. These designs strive to be as functional as possible. This particular bookcase has an enclosed lower section for concealed storage.

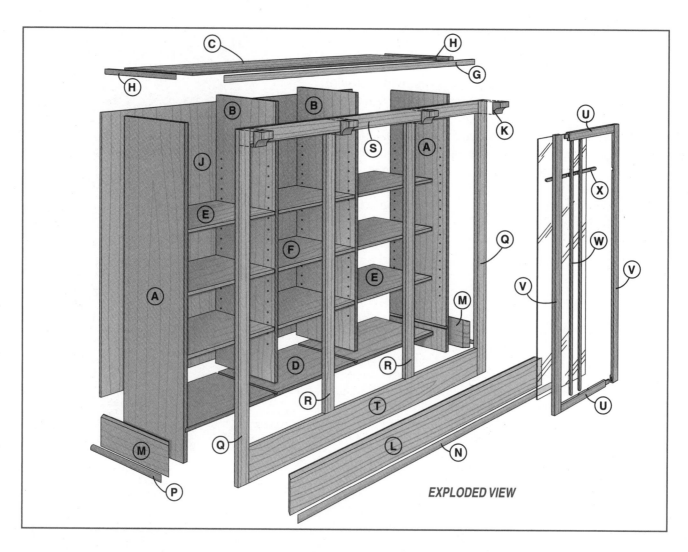

EXPLODED VIEW

MISSION BOOKCASE ■ MATERIALS LIST

PARTS

A	Sides* (2)	¾" x12" × 58½"
B	Dividers* (2)	¾" × 11¾" × 52⅞"
C	Top*	¾" × 14¼" × 56"
D	Bottom*	¾" × 11¾" × 55¼"
E	Adjustable outside shelves (3)	¾" × 11¾" × 17¾"
F	Adjustable middle shelves (6)	¾" × 11¾" × 17⅛"
G	Top trim front	¾" × 1½" × 57½"
H	Top trim sides (2)	¾" × 1½" × 15"
J	Back*	¼" × 55¼" × 53⅝"
K	Corbel (4)	1½" × 2½" × 2"
L	Bottom trim front	¾" × 5⅝" × 57½"
M	Bottom trim sides (2)	¾" × 5⅝" × 13½"
N	Bottom front molding	¾" × ¾" × 59"
P	Bottom side moldings (2)	¾" × ¾" × 14¼"

Q	Face frame outside stiles (2)	¾" × 2" × 58½"
R	Face frame middle stiles (2)	¾" × 2" × 50"
S	Face frame top rail	¾" × 2½" × 52"
T	Face frame bottom rail	¾" × 6" × 52"
U	Door rails (6)	¾" × 1½" × 16"
V	Door stiles (6)	¾" × 1½" 50"
W	Vertical muntins (6)	¼" × ⅝" × 48"
X	Horizontal muntins (3)	¼" × ⅝" × 14"

* Make these parts from plywood.

HARDWARE

No-mortise hinges (3 pair)	¾" × 1" × 2½"
Surface-mount locks (3)	⅜" thk. × 1⅝" tall × 1" wd.
Oval escutcheons (3)	⅝" × 2⅛"
Metal shelf pins (36)	¼" dia. × 1" lg.
Glass (3)	⅛" × 13⅞" × 47⅞"

How do I build it?

PREPARING THE MATERIALS

Chris made this bookcase from white oak and oak plywood, the wood of choice for Arts and Crafts craftsmen. Wherever he could, he used *quarter-sawn* stock; not just because it's more stable, but because quarter-sawn wood shows a formation known as *rays*. In white oak, these rays are extremely pronounced and produce a wonderful pattern that some craftsmen refer to as "silver grain."

In preparing the wood for this project, it's very important to make the frame members — the rails and stiles — perfectly straight. The doors on this cabinet are fairly large, and if the stiles are just a little bowed, the doors won't fit the case properly.

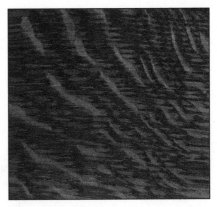

The "silver grain" figure in quarter-sawn white oak is due to the prominent rays running perpendicular to the wood grain.

Pick rough stock with relatively straight grain, bust it down into oversized parts to relieve any internal tensions, then follow the procedure I've outlined below in *Truing Lumber* to joint and plane it to size.

SHOP SAVVY ■ *Truing Lumber*

When making door frames and other cabinet parts that must be straight and true, how you prepare the wood is critical. No matter how accurately you lay out and cut the parts, it won't do you a bit of good if the lumber is poorly prepared. The parts will shrink, swell, cup, or bow after you've cut them, and all your careful craftsmanship will be for naught.

The first step in truing lumber is to let it *shop dry.* After purchasing the stock, let it rest in your shop for a week or two for each inch of thickness before working with it. The same holds for stock you've stored in a building separate from your shop. Resist the temptation to get to work immediately — you might have to do much of the job over again.

Remember, wood typically expands or contracts whenever you change its location, due to differences in relative humidity. When you first bring a board into your shop, it will be in motion. If you attempt to work it too soon, the surfaces that you plane perfectly flat today may be nothing to crow about by tomorrow.

To avoid problems, let the wood stabilize in its new environment. Stack it in a corner or on a rack until the moisture content of the wood has a chance to find an equilibrium with the humidity in your shop.

Once the wood has stabilized, you can joint and plane the surfaces straight, flat, and square to one another.

1 Begin by jointing one face of a board flat.

2 Turn the board 90 degrees so the jointed face rests against the fence, and joint one *edge* square to the jointed face.

3 Plane the remaining face parallel to the first.

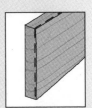

4 Finally, rip the remaining edge parallel to the other on a table saw. If you wish, cut the board 1/32 inch oversized, then joint the sawed edge to remove the saw marks.

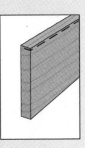

MAKING THE CASE

The case is a big plywood box— two sides, a fixed top, and a fixed bottom, joined with rabbets and dadoes. There are also two dividers inside the case, joined to the bottom and the top. These reduce the span of the shelves and help support the weight of the books.

The fixed shelves are joined to the sides with dadoes, and the back rests in rabbets at the back edges of the sides and top. The bottom ends of the

TRY THIS!

You can save some time by stacking the parts when you drill the shelving support holes. Stack one divider on one of the sides, and hold the parts together with double-faced carpet tape. Then drill through the divider and partway into the side. Repeat the process with the other divider and side.

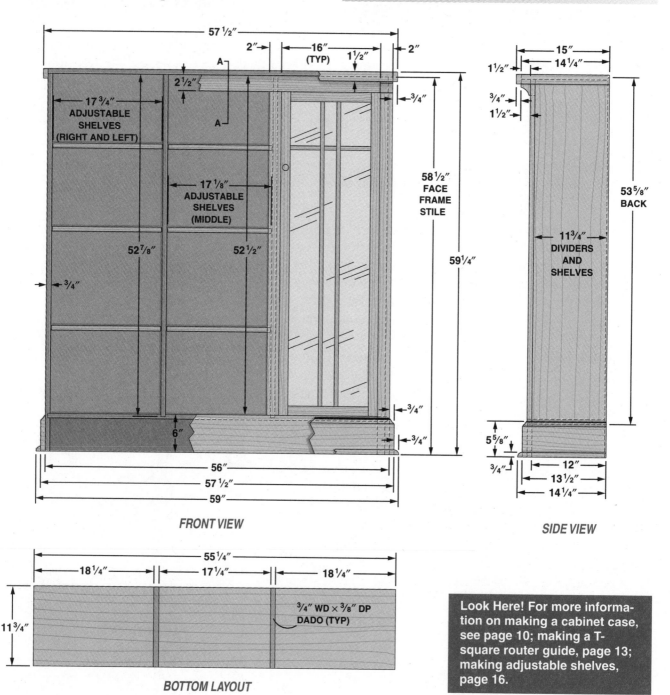

FRONT VIEW

SIDE VIEW

BOTTOM LAYOUT

Look Here! For more information on making a cabinet case, see page 10; making a T-square router guide, page 13; making adjustable shelves, page 16.

dividers rest in dadoes in the bottom shelf, and the top ends butt against the top held to it by pocket screws or dowels — all very simple construction. Chris cut the dadoes in the sides and the bottom shelf using a router and a T-Square Router Guide (page 13), then cut the rabbets on the table saw with a dado cutter.

The sides and the dividers support adjustable shelves on metal support pins. To install the pins, you must drill two rows of holes in each of the sides and in the dividers, as shown in the *Side Layout*. A Hole-Spacing Guide (page 17) makes short work of these holes.

Next edge the top with strips of solid wood to hide the plies. Miter the strips where they turn the front corners. The trim is usually saved for last, I know, but in this circumstance it's easier to do the edging *before* you attach the top. The edging also helps align the top to the sides during assembly.

SHOP SAVVY

The width of the face frame rails and stiles is very important to the appearance of the cabinet. If the frame members are too narrow, the cabinet looks frail. Too wide, and it looks clunky. For most cabinets this size, the width of the frame members are between 2 and 3 inches.

MAKING A FACE FRAME As I mentioned, this case has a face frame — rails and stiles that frame the door opening. This frame adds strength to the case, helping to keep the front opening rigid so the doors fit their opening properly. It also gives a cabinet a more traditional look. Most contemporary cabinets have no face frames.

Face Frame Joinery. There are several methods for joining the members of face frames. Traditionally, craftsmen used mortise-and-tenon joints or lap joints. These are overkill, however. You don't need super-strong joinery for this particular assembly. Face frames don't support that much weight.

So, many craftsmen use dowel joints instead. And more recently they have begun to use biscuit joints and pocket screws. I've tried all these variations and find that pocket screws are the fastest and easiest. They also seem to be strong enough to handle whatever stress you can put on a face frame. I've never had one come apart on me.

REPEAT HOLE LAYOUT ON DIVIDERS.

11⁷⁄₈″

10″

1″   1″

¼″ WD × ³⁄₈″ DP RABBET

2″ (TYP)

58½″

¼″ DIA × ½″ DP HOLES (TYP)

³⁄₄″ WD × ³⁄₈″ DP GROOVE

5¼″

12″

SIDE LAYOUT

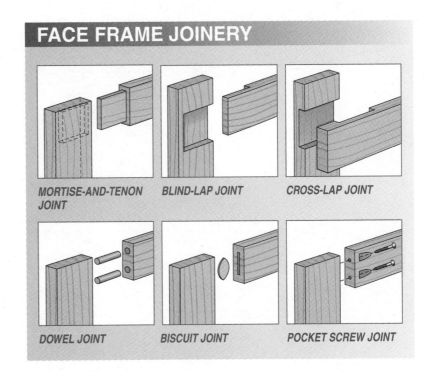

FACE FRAME JOINERY

MORTISE-AND-TENON JOINT

BLIND-LAP JOINT

CROSS-LAP JOINT

DOWEL JOINT

BISCUIT JOINT

POCKET SCREW JOINT

Pocket Screw Joints. To make a pocket screw joint, you must drive the screw through one part at a shallow angle. The screw exits the end of that part and bites into the edge of an adjoining part. The head of the screw rests in a pocket.

The trick is to drill the pockets and drive the screws at the proper angle. To do this, you need a special *stepped bit* — it drills the pilot hole and the pocket hole at the same time — and a guide to keep the bit at the proper angle.

To make pocket screw joints, you need a special bit and a guide to position it. These are available through most woodworking supply companies.

QUICK FIXTURE ■ *Pocket Screw Jig*

To use a pocket screw guide, you must clamp it to the wood. Additionally, it must be properly aligned with the end of the board. This fixture holds the drill guide and aligns it for you. To use it, attach the guide to the edge of the mount with a lag screw. Most guides already have mounting holes. If yours doesn't, you must drill one. Be careful that you don't drill through the angled guide hole as you do.

Position the stop board on the mount — the L-shaped stop cradles the work, holding the end of each board in the same position next to the guide. Clamp the stop and the mount in a vise. Rest a board in the stop and clamp it to the guide. Check that the guide is correctly positioned on the work, then drill the pocket and shank hole.

The chamfer on the edges of the stop gives the sawdust somewhere to go, and keeps it from interfering with the position of the stock in the jig.

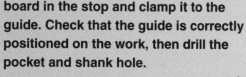

2¼″

³⁄₈″ CHAMFERS

7″

3½″

1″ DIA

11¾″

STOP

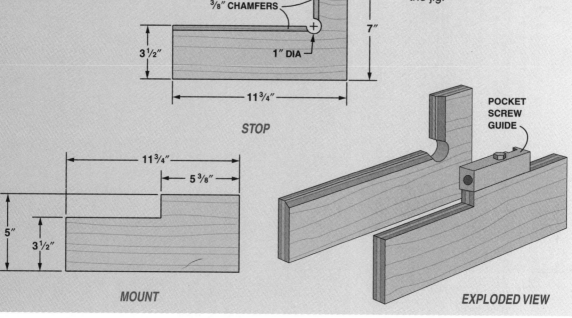

11¾″

5 ³⁄₈″

5″

3½″

MOUNT

POCKET SCREW GUIDE

EXPLODED VIEW

METHODS OF WORK ■ *Making Pocket Screw Joints*

P ocket screws are an effective, simple method for joining supported frames — frames that are sustained by a larger structure. Face frames, for example, are supported by a case. However, don't use pocket screws for nonsupported frames (such as doors) or load-bearing frames (such as web frames).

When assembling frames, drill the pockets and shank holes in the ends of the members, where they butt against the edges of the adjoining parts. When you drive the screws, they must bite into long grain on the adjoining member. They will not hold in end grain.

1 Arrange the parts in the configuration that you want to join them. If necessary, clamp them together. Mark the location of each pocket screw across the seam between the adjoining parts.

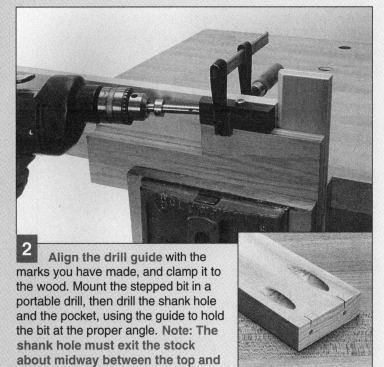

2 Align the drill guide with the marks you have made, and clamp it to the wood. Mount the stepped bit in a portable drill, then drill the shank hole and the pocket, using the guide to hold the bit at the proper angle. Note: The shank hole must exit the stock about midway between the top and bottom faces. Additionally, the pocket should stop ½ to ¾ inch before the end of the board. If the pilot hole isn't where it should be, adjust the position of the guide on the work. If the pocket is too long or too short, adjust the stop on the drill bit.

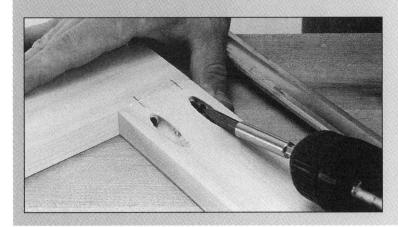

3 Apply glue to the mating surfaces, align the layout marks, and clamp the parts together. Drive roundhead drywall screws through the pockets into the edge of the adjoining part. These roundhead screws are available through the same stores and outlets that sell pocket screw guides.

MAKING GLAZED DOORS

The glazed doors on this bookcase are *inset* in the face frame. The outside faces of the doors are flush with the outside faces of the frame. Although they appear to have several panes of glass, each door has just one. The *muntins* — the vertical and horizontal strips of wood inside the door frame — are laid over the glass panel.

> **Look Here!** For more information on types of doors, see page 20.

MAKING THE DOOR JOINERY The door frame members are joined with through mortises and tenons. The tenons extend completely through the stiles. There are two reasons for this, one practical and one aesthetic. The practical reason is that the longer the tenons, the more gluing surface there is in the joints. And the more gluing surface, the stronger the joints will be.

The aesthetic reason is that the mission style often uses *frank* joinery. This means that the craftsman makes no attempt to hide his joinery. The tenons are not "blind," hidden in stopped mortises. The mortises and tenons go all the way

SHOP SAVVY

When making mortise-and-tenon joints, make the mortise first, then fit the tenon to it. It's much more difficult to fit the mortise around the tenon.

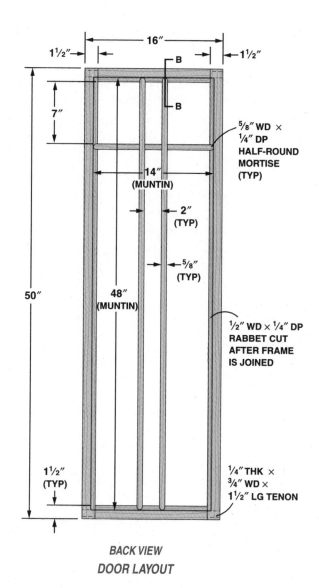

16"
1½"   1½"
B
7"
B
5/8" WD ×
¼" DP
HALF-ROUND
MORTISE
(TYP)
14"
(MUNTIN)
2"
(TYP)
5/8"
(TYP)
50"
48"
(MUNTIN)
½" WD × ¼" DP
RABBET CUT
AFTER FRAME
IS JOINED
¼" THK ×
¾" WD ×
1½" LG TENON
1½"
(TYP)

BACK VIEW
DOOR LAYOUT

To make a through mortise on the joint maker, you must work from both sides. Clamp the stile in the carriage so the edge is perpendicular to the bit. Rout halfway through the stock, plunging the work into the bit. Then turn the board face for face and repeat on the opposite edge.

To make tenons on the joint maker, use a large straight bit, ¾ inch or more in diameter. Mount the rails in the carriage so the edges are parallel to the bit. Feed the work over the bit, cutting against the rotation.

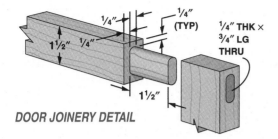

DOOR JOINERY DETAIL

1/4"
(TYP)
1/4" THK ×
3/4" LG
THRU
1 1/2"
1/4"
1/4"
1 1/2"

through the boards so you can see them. Mission furniture makers considered frank joinery a mark of honest craftsmanship. In later mission pieces, the designers use visible joinery as a design element.

Chris routed the through mortises in the stiles using a fixture very much like the Joint Maker on page 114. (In fact, it was one of its prototypes.) Note that he left the ends of the mortises round and rounded the surfaces of the tenons to match, as shown in the *Door Joinery Detail.* This is simple enough to do; just give the tenons a couple of licks with a cabinetmaker's rasp to round over the arrises. Of course, you can do it the other way and square the ends of the mortise with a chisel to

match the tenon. It all depends on whether or not you want your tenons to appear frankly rounded or frankly square.

When you're satisfied with the fit of the door frame joints, assemble the frames with glue. *Make absolutely certain the frames are flat and square as you glue them up.*

OOPS!

If, after assembly, the case isn't square or the face frame isn't flat, you must compensate for that when you glue up the door frames. After Chris installed these bookcases in my crooked old Victorian home, there wasn't a square opening or a flat surface to be seen. So he glued up the door frames *in the cases!* He fit each door to its opening *before* final assembly. Then, immediately after gluing the parts together, he wedged the doors in their openings with toothpicks. Like the case, the doors dried out of square. But they fit perfectly.

NO PROBLEM ■ *Fitting Mortises and Tenons*

You think you've cut your tenons to fit your mortises perfectly, but when you put them together, the gaps are big enough to drive a truck through. No problem. To correct a sloppy

fit in a mortise-and-tenon joint, make some shims from scraps of veneer. If the tenon will be visible on the assembled joint, match the wood grain and color of the veneer to the tenon.

1 Glue veneer shims to *both* cheeks of the tenon. You may also have to attach shims to the top and bottom surfaces of the tenons. Let the glue dry.

2 If the shims make the tenon too tight in the mortise, shave them down with a router plane. Shave opposing shims the same amount — you want the tenon to remain centered in the mortise.

Look Here! For more information on router planes, see page 25.

ROUTING A GLASS RABBET The glass panes rest in rabbets in the inside edges of the door frames. I usually cut these rabbets *after* I assemble the frame, then cut the corners square with a chisel. I noticed that Chris elected to do it this way when he made these doors. There are joints especially designed for glazed doors that require you to cut the rabbet as you make the frame joinery. When the frames go together, the rabbet is already in place. The rabbeted frame mortise-and-tenon joint is the most common of these, and it will work well for the bookcase doors if you'd rather use it. Both techniques are equally effective.

If you want to give the door a more finished look when it's open, add a *glass bead* to the inside. This little molding acts as a keeper for the glass pane. If you do elect to use a bead, make the glass rabbet deep enough to accept both the glass and the bead.

Don't install the glass yet. Wait until after you have completed the bookcase and applied a finish. It's very difficult to finish the wooden frame on a glazed door with the glass in place.

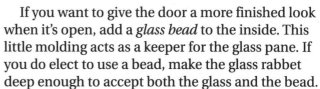

TRY THIS!

When it is time to install the glass, secure it in the rabbet with silicone caulk. Jim taught me this trick, and it's much easier and stronger than brads or glazing points. You can also use the caulk to hold the glass bead in place, if you've elected to make it.

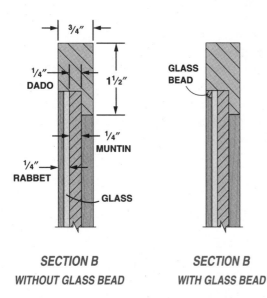

SECTION B
WITHOUT GLASS BEAD

SECTION B
WITH GLASS BEAD

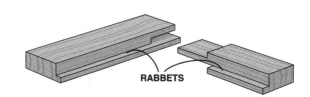

RABBETED-FRAME
MORTISE-AND-TENON JOINT

To keep the router from tipping as you rabbet the narrow rails and stiles, secure a scrap of molding to the sole with double-faced carpet tape. After routing, cut the corners square with a chisel.

A glass bead makes a door look finished inside and out. Attach this molding to the shoulder of the glass rabbet. Miter the bead where it turns a corner.

MAKING MUNTINS Classic furniture (Queen Anne, Chippendale, and Federal styles) often has framed doors fitted with muntins. These are small rails and stiles — usually smaller than the outside frame members — with glass rabbets on the back. They divide the glazing opening into smaller sections. Classic cabinetmakers did it this way because there just weren't any large panes of glass before the 1850s. Today, there's no practical reason to make muntins except for looks.

Traditional muntins are assembled with coped mortises and tenons or *sash joints.* The structural integrity is important because the assembly must support the weight of several panes of glass. Consequently, you must join, fit, and glue the muntins together.

Decorative muntins — like the ones on the bookcase doors — are much simpler to make. These are strips of wood, rounded at the ends.

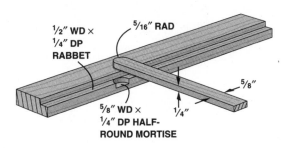

MUNTIN FRAME JOINERY

Chris used a drill bit to make half-round mortises in the inside shoulders of the glass rabbets, then fitted the rounded ends of the muntins to them. (If he had wanted to, he could have squared the corners of the mortises with a chisel and simply laid the strips in place without rounding the ends.) Where the muntins crossed one another, he cut lap joints.

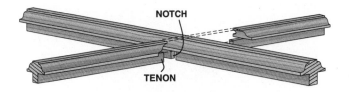

TRADITIONAL SASH JOINT, JOINING 2 MUNTINS

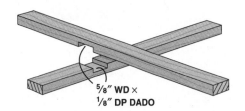

MUNTIN JOINERY DETAIL

Cut the half-round mortises in the door frames with a Forstner bit. (This type of drill bit cuts a flat bottom in the hole.)

Cut the lap joints in the muntins on a table saw, using a dado cutter. Each joint consists of two matched dadoes. **Tip: If you're making a lot of doors, as Chris did, cut dadoes in a wide board, then rip the muntins from it.**

HANGING THE DOORS

Chris opted to hang the doors in this bookcase with no-mortise hinges (also called flush hinges). These have thin leaves, no more than 1/16 inch thick, that fold into one another. Consequently, the hinges are about as thick as the gap you'd normally leave between the door frame and the face frame when you fit the doors. This, in turn, means that you don't have to cut mortises for these hinges. Just mark the positions on the doors and case, then install them with screws.

Look Here! For more information on hanging doors, see page 25.

To hang a cabinet door on no-mortise hinges, begin the same way you would if you were using butt hinges. Wedge the door in place in the cabinet, and mark the position of the hinges across both the door frame and the case.

Position each hinge at the marks with the leaves folded over the arris, then drill the screw holes with a Vix bit.

ALTERNATIVES ■ *Cabinet Door Hinges*

There are many different hinges you might use on a cabinet door, depending on its design and how it fits the case. Here are a few of the more popular types.

Butt Hinge
General-purpose, for inset and overlay doors

Loose-Pin Hinge
General-purpose, for inset and overlay doors that must be removed from time to time

No-Mortise Hinge
Light- to medium-duty, for inset and overlay doors

Offset Hinge
For lipped doors only, bent leaf fits around door lip

European Cabinet Hinge
General-purpose, typically used for inset and overlay doors on cabinets without face frames, but there are special hinges available for face-frame constructions as well.

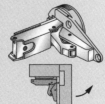

Knife Hinge
Light-duty, recessed into top and bottom edges of doors

Piano Hinge
Heavy-duty, typically used for doors that must support a great deal of weight. Available in lengths up to 6 feet.

INSTALLING THE DOOR LATCHES To open and close the bookcase doors, Chris chose traditional locking latches — in this arrangement, the keys serve as knobs to open the doors, and the lock holds it closed. Although many cabinet locks require you to cut mortises in both the door and the frame, this particular latch (called a surface-mounted cupboard lock) does not. (I don't know what it was about this project — Chris seemed to have avoided cutting hardware mortises like the plague.)

To install each latch, drill a hole in the door stile large enough for the key to fit through. Secure the latch to the inside surface of the door with screws, then install a key escutcheon on the outside surface to protect and dress up the key hole. When you turn the key, the locking bar slips behind the face frame stile, holding the door closed.

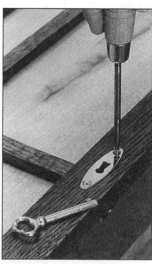

A surface-mounted cupboard lock *(left)* requires no mortise. But with a decorative escutcheon *(right)*, it looks just as handsome as the mortised variety.

CONSIDER THIS!

This latching system may not be a good idea if you have small children, especially ones with odd senses of humor. They hide the keys.

To make a "key hole," you must cut a short slot. The easiest way I've found to do this is to drill two holes next to one another, then angle the drill bit back and forth to cut away the waste between them. If necessary, you can clean up the edges of the hole with a small file.

LATCHES FOR DOUBLE DOORS If you design your bookcase with double doors (two doors in the same opening), you'll need to use a slightly different latch arrangement. First of all, make the door so the inside stile on one door is slightly wider than its neighbor. In this stile, cut a rabbet in the outside arris. On the other door, cut a matching rabbet in the inside arris of the inside stile. When the doors are closed, the rabbets should lap over one another with the wide stile behind the narrower one.

Install an elbow catch to hold the door with the wide stile closed. Mount the catch on the inside face of the wide stile, and mount the plate that it catches onto a fixed shelf or some other permanent part of the case. Finally install a locking latch in the other door. When the wide-stile door is closed and the elbow catch is engaged, the latch bar will slide behind the wide stile. This will keep both doors closed. To open them, simply turn the key, swing the narrow-stile door open, and disengage the elbow catch. Neat, huh?

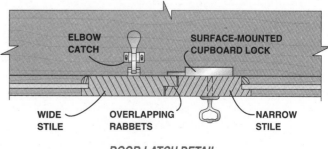

ELBOW CATCH   SURFACE-MOUNTED CUPBOARD LOCK

WIDE STILE   OVERLAPPING RABBETS   NARROW STILE

DOOR LATCH DETAIL

MAKING AND INSTALLING THE CORBELS

To add a little decoration to the top of the bookcase, Mary Jane added some corbels, an old Gothic device that was originally intended as an architectural brace. These, of course, don't brace anything — they are simply decorative *appliqués*.

Chris installed the corbels by gluing them to the face frame, as shown in *Section A*. The corbels are aligned with — and are the same width as — the stiles in the face frame.

> **Look Here!** For more information on making and attaching appliqués, see page 110.

To make the corbels, cut the coves with a band saw or coping saw. The wood grain in the corbels should run *horizontally* when they are attached to the bookcase.

FINISHING THE BOOKCASE

Once you've reached this point, you can begin thinking about applying a finish. What finish you apply will depend on a dozen factors that I can't anticipate, but I'll tell you what I used on the off chance it may come in handy.

I finish-sanded the wooden surface to 180 grit, then wet down the entire cabinet with a damp rag to raise the grain and the "whiskers," loose wood fibers that stand up when you apply a finish, creating dimples and heartbreaks. Oak is notorious for its whiskers. But a little water takes care of the problem — the whiskers stand up and you can knock them off with a light sanding after the surface dries.

Raising the grain is also important if you plan to apply a water-based stain, which is what I did next. If you don't raise the grain beforehand, the water in the stain will cause the wood fibers to swell and the surfaces will be uneven. You have to sand it down a second time to make it smooth. In doing so, you may sand away more stain in one area than in another, and the color will appear uneven.

After sanding the raised grain smooth, I applied an aniline dye. This enhances the silver grain in the white oak. The rays don't accept the stain as well as the long grain; consequently they stay fairly light. This increases the contrast between the two types of grain and makes the rays pop.

Once the aniline dye was dry, I covered it with a "wash coat" — a 1-pound cut — of white shellac. On occasion, I've had an aniline dye bleed through a finish (especially through penetrating finishes), but shellac prevents any bleeding by sealing in the dye.

Finally, I applied several coats of a wipe-on tung oil finish mixed with a dab of spar varnish. This is a trick I learned from master turner Rude Osolnik. Rude mixes about a tablespoon of varnish to a cup of tung oil. It's still a wipe-on finish, but it builds to a gloss much faster and is much more durable than straight tung oil.

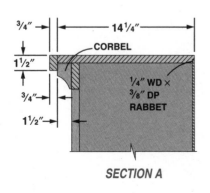

SECTION A

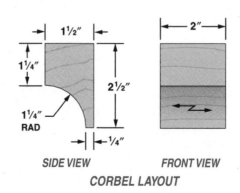

SIDE VIEW / FRONT VIEW
CORBEL LAYOUT

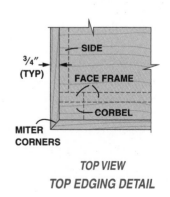

TOP VIEW
TOP EDGING DETAIL

METHODS OF WORK ■ *Installing Glass Doors*

Glass doors (as opposed to *glazed* doors) are solid sheets of glass; they have no wooden frame. Use ¼-inch-thick glass for these; thinner glass doesn't have sufficient strength to be safe. Most glass suppliers have specific types of glass that they recommend for doors.

Have the doors cut after you build the cabinet. Dimensions have a way of creeping as you assemble the parts, and door openings magically get larger or smaller than you had planned. Measure the openings, and have the doors cut to fit.

Also have the edges of the glass polished. This is expensive, but it's worth the money. The cut edge of a glass plate is extremely sharp, and you (or your loved ones) could cut yourself badly just by opening a door.

Glass doors require special hardware to hang them. All of the hinges, latches, and pulls shown can be installed without drilling or cutting the glass.

Most glass-door hinges hold the plate glass in channels. Occasionally, there are screws on the back of the hinge to lock the glass in place; but more often, the hinge is held with adhesive or tape. The hinge pivots on a plate (which is screwed to a horizontal surface) or a bracket (which is attached to a vertical surface).

The easiest way to hold a glass door closed is with a magnetic latch. Slip a strike plate over one corner of the door, and mount a magnet behind it.

You can also purchase clip-on pulls. Like the magnetic strike plates, these slip over the edge of the glass door and are secured with adhesive or tape. Note: If you use a magnetic touch latch, you won't need a pull to open and close the door.

SHOP SAVVY

Should you need to drill a hole in a glass door to install a knob or another piece of hardware, purchase a special carbide drill bit designed for this purpose. Using putty, build up a dam around the area where you will drill the hole, and keep it filled with kerosene or mineral oil as you drill. This keeps the glass cool so it won't crack.

RESOURCES

Purchase glass-door hardware from:
The Woodworkers' Store
4365 Willow Drive
Medina, MN 55340

ALTERNATIVES ■ *Making Built-Ins*

What if you want to *build in* the bookcase, attaching it to the wall as Chris did? The differences between stand-alone cabinets and built-ins are not large. Built-in cabinets have a horizontal *nailing strip* or *hanging strip* across the back. This strip is located at the back, just beneath the top or the counter. It strengthens the back where it's attached to the wall. For counter units, it provides additional support for the countertops at the wall.

They may also have a *fitting allowance* — extra stock at the back edges of the sides and sometimes the base. If the cabinet has a face frame, the outside edges of the face frame stiles may extend a fraction of an inch beyond the side, creating a fitting allowance there as well. When you install the cabinets, you trim this allowance to fit irregular walls and floors.

Cabinets that are designed to serve as *work centers* as well as storage pieces often have recessed *toe spaces* at the floor. This prevents you from stubbing your toes as you stand at the cabinet and work. Additionally, the work surface or *counter* is often made as a separate piece and attached after the cabinet has been installed.

CABINET UNITS Built-in cabinet systems also tend to be much larger than stand-alone cabinets. The mission bookcases, for example, occupy an entire wall in my living room. To make them easy to handle, they are *modular* — made up of cabinet units arranged like building blocks to fit the space.

There are three basic types of units:

■ A counter unit rests on the floor and has a waist-high work surface. The bathroom vanity is a counter unit.

■ A wall unit hangs on a wall at eye level.

■ A tall unit rests on the floor and extends above counter height (about 36 inches), often to within a few inches of the ceiling. The bookcase is a tall unit.

Most units are simple rectangles. But when you want to turn a corner with a unit, you must make it either L-shaped or five-sided.

This built-in kitchen cabinet system consists of 12 modules — 5 counter units, 6 wall units, and 1 tall unit. Two of the counter units have 5 sides to turn a corner.

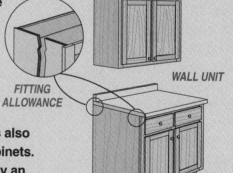

FITTING ALLOWANCE

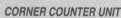

WALL UNIT

CORNER WALL UNIT

COUNTER UNIT

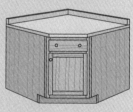

CORNER COUNTER UNIT

TALL UNIT

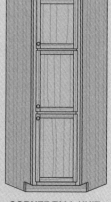

CORNER TALL UNIT

STANDARD BUILT-IN UNITS

STANDARD BUILT-IN CABINET DIMENSIONS

These dimensions are intended as guidelines only. Design the complete built-in assembly to fit the available space, and size the individual units so they're easy to handle and to install.

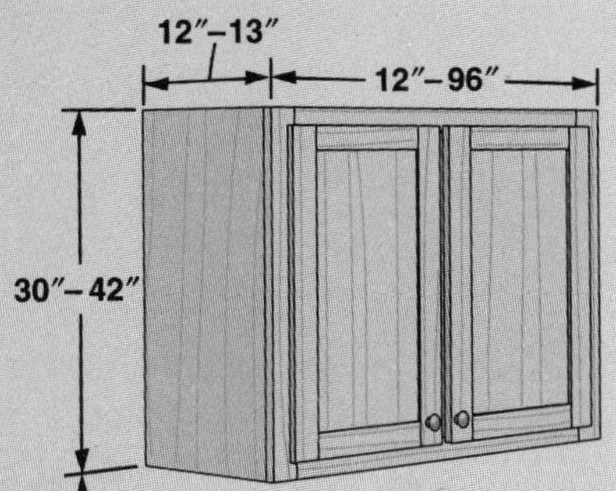

12"–13"

12"–96"

30"–42"

WALL UNIT

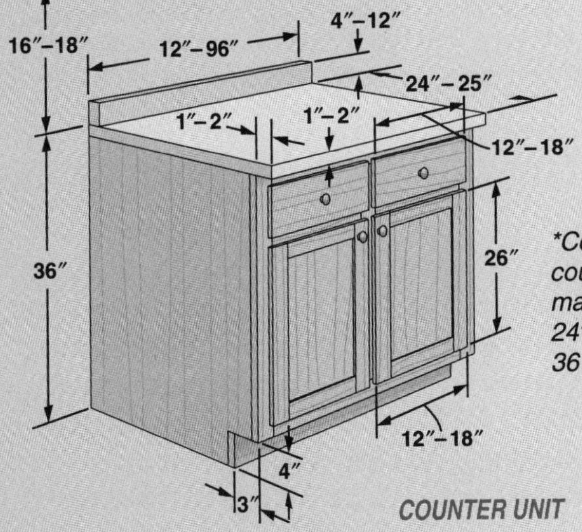

16"–18"

12"–96"

4"–12"

24"–25"

1"–2"

1"–2"

12"–18"

36"

26"

Commercial countertops are made to fit units 24", 30", and 36" deep.

12"–18"

4"

3"

COUNTER UNIT

23"–24"

25"

12"–25"

12"–96"

60"–84"

5"–6"

6"–10"

10"–12"

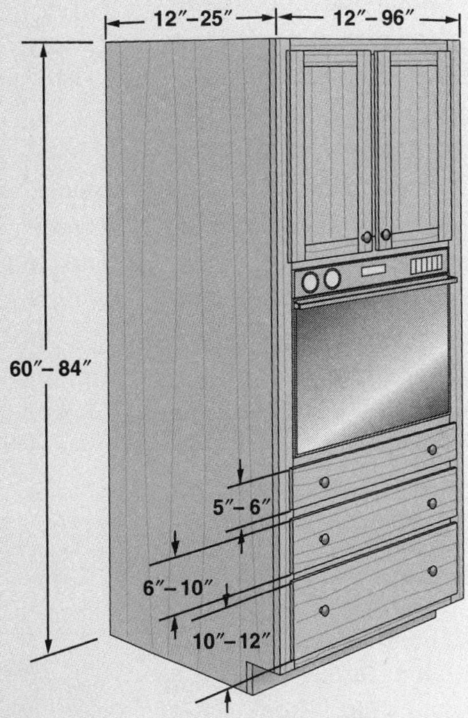

TALL UNIT

(Drawer width often matches door above or below.)

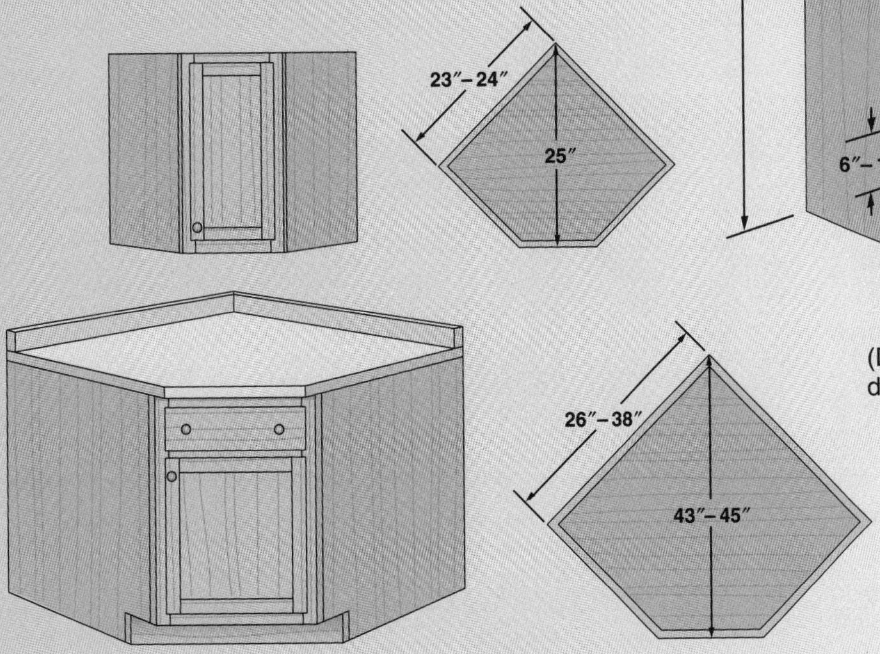

26"–38"

43"–45"

CORNER UNITS

(continued on next page)

ALTERNATIVES ■ *Making Built-Ins* — CONTINUED

INSTALLING A BUILT-IN CABINET To install a built-in, you must attach it directly to the structure of the building. If the walls are made of masonry, bolt each unit in place using lag screws and expandable lead anchors. If they're made of plaster or dry-wall on a wood frame, screw the cabinets to the studs in the wall. Drive the fasteners through the nailing strips.

To attach cabinets to the studs in the wall, first you have to locate the studs. A stud sensor works well; I've also had great luck with the old "hunt-and-peck" method. Tap with a hammer, listening to the sound. A low-pitched hollow sound means you're between the studs. As you tap nearer to a stud, the pitch rises and the sound becomes

After you have positioned the cabinet units and you are satisfied that they are level, fasten the sides together with wood screws. If two adjoining cabinets have a fitting allowance at the face frame, place shims between the sides. After the cabinets are joined, trim the shims flush with the top edges of the sides.

more "solid." I always drill several small holes to make sure I've found the stud. Afterward, I fill the holes with spackle.

Once you've found the studs, set the units in place. Check that the units are level, the fronts are

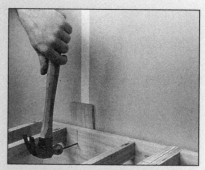

If the back of the cabinet stands out from the wall slightly, place shims between the back and the wall. Fasten each cabinet unit to the wall with 16d nails or 3-inch-long wood screws, driving the fasteners through the nailing strips and shims, then into the wall studs. Afterward, trim the shims flush with the top edges.

flush with one another, and the top edges are all at the same level. Attach the cabinet units to each other first, then drive screws through the nailing strips and into the studs in the wall.

QUICK FIXTURE ■ *Dead Man*

To hang a wall unit, make one or more dead men to rest it on while you drive the fasteners through the nailing strips. A dead man is a T-shaped fixture, made from scraps of 2 × 4's and plywood. Cut the supporting member to the length needed to hold the cabinet at the proper height. Have a helper steady the cabinet on the dead men while you fasten it to the wall.

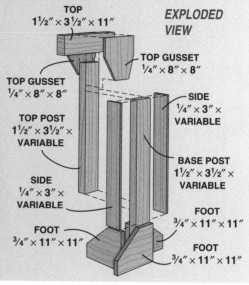

EXPLODED VIEW

TOP
1½″ × 3½″ × 11″

TOP GUSSET
¼″ × 8″ × 8″

TOP GUSSET
¼″ × 8″ × 8″

SIDE
¼″ × 3″ × VARIABLE

TOP POST
1½″ × 3½″ × VARIABLE

BASE POST
1½″ × 3½″ × VARIABLE

SIDE
¼″ × 3″ × VARIABLE

FOOT
¾″ × 11″ × 11″

FOOT
¾″ × 11″ × 11″

FOOT
¾″ × 11″ × 11″

NO PROBLEM ■ *Leveling a Cabinet*

You measure the space for your built-in cabinet as carefully as possible, build the cabinet to exacting tolerances, and put it in place — and it rests at an angle, teetering on the floor and barely making contact with the back wall. Believe it or not, this is no problem — as long as you've left yourself some *fitting allowance*.

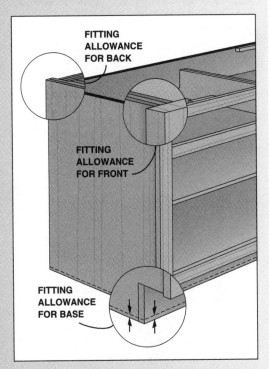

FITTING ALLOWANCE FOR BACK

FITTING ALLOWANCE FOR FRONT

FITTING ALLOWANCE FOR BASE

1   **Shim the bottom** of the cabinet so the top edges are level, side to side and front to back.

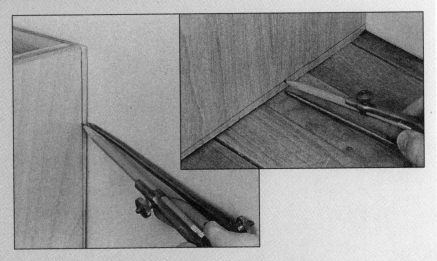

2   **Adjust a compass** so the distance between the point and the scribe is equal to the widest gap between the cabinet and the wall. Place the point of the compass against the wall and trace its surface, scribing the contour onto the side of the cabinet. Repeat at the bottom of the cabinet, tracing the contour of the floor.

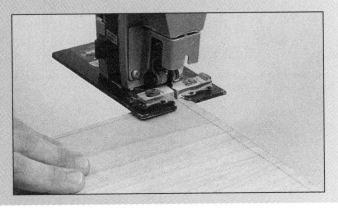

3   **Carefully trim the sides and bottom** along the lines you have scribed. When you set the cabinet in place again, it will butt solidly against the wall and rest perfectly level on the floor.

Chippendale China Cabinet

I've used the term *cabinet* in its broadest sense in this book to encompass cupboards, bookcases, and similar storage pieces. A true cabinet, however, is a very specific piece of furniture. In the sixteenth century, Europe began to import fine porcelain from the Orient. So folks could display these treasures, woodworkers (who called themselves *joiners* in those days) developed a cupboard with glazed doors. The French called this a *cabinette* (which the English shortened to "cabinet"), after the word for cabin, a one-room house with windows.

That being so, this is the only true cabinet in this book. And what a cabinet! I made the walnut case many years ago and neglected to finish it for the simple reason that, like most woodworkers, I collect incomplete projects. When this book came around, Jim and I judged it was properly aged, so we blew off the dust. Mary Jane wrinkled up her nose at my original design and convinced me that with some additional work, my old case might amount to something. And it did, as you can see. Jim built the classic base and top and completed the cabinet. And I — well, I let him.

Despite its elegant appearance, the china cabinet has a good deal in common with the previous projects in this book. At its core, it's an ordinary rectangular case with a face frame. The bottom portion is enclosed with frame-and-panel doors (like the spice cupboard), while the top section has glazed doors (like the mission bookcase). There are, however, several new components. The case sits on a *frame base* and is capped with a *pediment top*. And there is a drawer between the top and bottom sections that rests on a *web frame*.

What size should it be?

Again, that depends on what you have to store. Not all china cabinets are used to store china. This cabinet could easily serve as a display case for any number of small and medium-size collectibles. In fact, Jim outfitted the top section of the cabinet with glass shelves just for that purpose. The glass doesn't block the light, and it lets you see the items on the shelves more easily.

If you use the cabinet to store plates and saucers, the shelves should be at least 12 to 13 inches wide to accommodate a full-size dinner plate. Other items might require wider shelves. Ordinarily, cabinets are between 12 and 24 inches deep. They vary in width from 30 inches to 66 inches and in height from 70 inches to 84 inches. This particular piece is a little taller, but Mary Jane figured we could get away with it because it stands in a room with 10-foot ceilings.

Believe it or not, the sophisticated china cabinet evolved from a primitive shelving unit, much like this reproduction "pewter bench." These wooden racks were used in medieval times to display a nobleman's "plate" or dinnerware. The number of shelves in the rack showed his rank, and the quality of his plate indicated his success. Later craftsmen added doors and drawers and made it larger and heavier.

What shape should it be?

More to the point, how do you want the cabinet to be shaped? As designed, the china cabinet is just a large, vertical case with some ornate stuff on the top and bottom. But many china cabinets have a step-back: The top portion of the case is shallower than the bottom portion. This allows you to use the fixed shelf at waist height as a serving counter — the cabinet doubles as a sideboard.

If you have a lot of dishes or a taste for elegance, what about a breakfront? This shape is actually three standing cases joined side by side. The two flanking cases are shallower than the middle one. This really fills up a room.

Finally, depending on where you want to place the cabinet in your home, you might want to consider making a corner cabinet. This type of piece usually has a pentagonal, or five-sided, footprint. When resting in a corner, the front of the cabinet is 45 degrees to the adjoining walls.

STEP-BACK CABINET

Courtesy of The Colonial Williamsburg Foundation, Williamsburg, VA

BREAKFRONT CABINET

CORNER CABINET

STANDARD CHINA CABINET SIZES

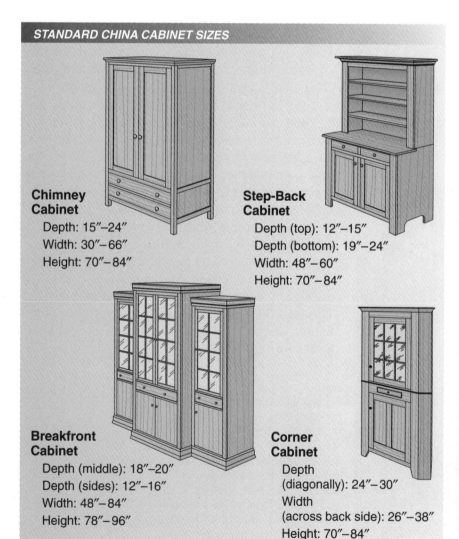

Chimney Cabinet
Depth: 15"–24"
Width: 30"–66"
Height: 70"–84"

Step-Back Cabinet
Depth (top): 12"–15"
Depth (bottom): 19"–24"
Width: 48"–60"
Height: 70"–84"

Breakfront Cabinet
Depth (middle): 18"–20"
Depth (sides): 12"–16"
Width: 48"–84"
Height: 78"–96"

Corner Cabinet
Depth (diagonally): 24"–30"
Width (across back side): 26"–38"
Height: 70"–84"

What style will it be?

As shown, the china cabinet is designed in the American Chippendale style. Thomas Chippendale, an eighteenth-century English architect, published a "pattern book" in 1754 called *The Gentleman and Cabinet-Maker's Director.* It's full of ornate furniture designs based on earlier Queen Anne-style designs, but heavier and more decorated. His designs were widely used on both sides of the Atlantic, although the American interpretation of Chippendale forms is much more restrained than Thomas probably would have liked.

If Chippendale isn't your cup of tea, you can easily change the style, yet keep the same basic construction. Here are a few examples.

Crafted by Larry Templeton, Dallas, TX; photo by Cutter-Smith Photographics

COUNTRY STYLE

Country cabinetmakers — craftsmen who built furniture along classic lines for common folks in the eighteenth and nineteenth centuries, often painted their furniture. In this reproduction by David T. Smith, the paint imitates a highly figured wood grain. Since their clients couldn't afford exotic materials, country craftsmen sometimes painted an attractive grain pattern over inexpensive wood.

STUDIO STYLE

The Studio or Handicraft Revival style is the newest of furniture styles. Its most striking characteristic is technique. Studio craftsmen have invented many new techniques and have pushed traditional methods to new frontiers. This cabinet is a good example. The book-matched veneered panels and the leaded glass that echo them show highly developmental design skill and method.

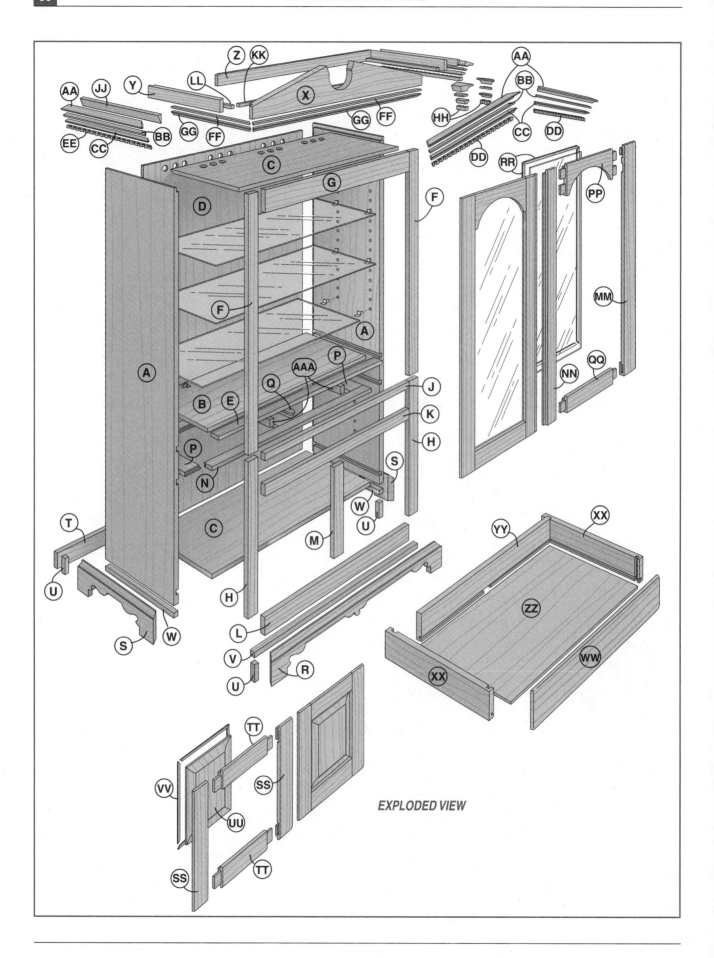

EXPLODED VIEW

CHIPPENDALE CHINA CABINET ■ MATERIALS LIST

PARTS

A	Sides (2)	$3/4'' \times 14^{1}/4'' \times 75^{1}/4''$
B	Counter	$3/4'' \times 14'' \times 33^{1}/4''$
C	Top/bottom	$3/4'' \times 14^{1}/4'' \times 33^{1}/4''$
D	Back*	$1/4'' \times 33^{1}/4'' \times 72^{3}/4''$
E	Counter edge	$3/4'' \times 1^{3}/4'' \times 34''$
F	Upper face frame stiles (2)	$3/4'' \times 2'' \times 46''$
G	Upper face frame rail	$3/4'' \times 2^{1}/2'' \times 30''$
H	Lower face frame stiles (2)	$3/4'' \times 2'' \times 28^{1}/2''$
J	Lower face frame top rail	$3/4'' \times 1^{1}/4'' \times 30''$
K	Lower face frame middle rail	$3/4'' \times 2'' \times 30''$
L	Lower face frame bottom rail	$3/4'' \times 2^{1}/2'' \times 30''$
M	Lower face frame mullion	$3/4'' \times 2'' \times 18^{3}/4''$
N	Web frame stiles (2)	$3/4'' \times 2'' \times 33^{1}/4''$
P	Web frame rails (3)	$3/4'' \times 3'' \times 10^{3}/4''$
Q	Guide	$1/4'' \times 1'' \times 14''$
	Optional wood shelves (not shown)	$3/4'' \times 11'' \times 32^{1}/4''$
R	Base front	$3/4'' \times 5'' \times 35^{1}/2''$
S	Base sides (2)	$3/4'' \times 5'' \times 15^{3}/4''$
T	Base back	$3/4'' \times 4'' \times 34''$
U	Base corner blocks (4)	$3/4'' \times 3/4'' \times 4''$
V	Horizontal front cleat	$3/4'' \times 3/4'' \times 34''$
W	Horizontal side cleats (2)	$3/4'' \times 3/4'' \times 13^{1}/2''$
X	Pediment front	$1^{1}/8'' \times 7^{7}/16'' \times 34^{3}/4''$
Y	Pediment sides (2)	$3/4'' \times 2^{5}/16'' \times 14^{13}/16''$
Z	Pediment back	$3/4'' \times 2^{5}/16'' \times 34''$
AA	Top ogee molding (total)	$3/4'' \times 1^{3}/8'' \times 84''$
BB	Top half-round molding (total)	$1/4'' \times 3/4'' \times 84''$
CC	Top cove molding (total)	$1/2'' \times 5/8'' \times 84''$
DD	Front dentil molding (total)	$1/4'' \times 1/2'' \times 40''$
EE	Side dentil molding (total)	$1/4'' \times 1/2'' \times 36''$
FF	Bottom half-round molding (total)	$1/4'' \times 1/2'' \times 72''$
GG	Bottom ogee molding (total)	$3/8'' \times 1/2'' \times 72''$
HH	Return dentil molding (total)	$1/4'' \times 5/8'' \times 12''$
JJ	Wedges (2)	$17/32'' \times 1^{1}/2'' \times 15^{3}/8''$
KK	Front cleat	$3/4'' \times 3/4'' \times 34''$
LL	Side cleats (2)	$3/4'' \times 3/4'' \times 13^{1}/2''$
MM	Upper door outer stiles (2)	$3/4'' \times 3'' \times 44^{5}/16''$
NN	Upper door inner stiles (2)	$3/4'' \times 2^{3}/16'' \times 44^{5}/16''$
PP	Upper door top rails (2)	$3/4'' \times 7'' \times 13^{1}/4''$
QQ	Upper door bottom rails (2)	$3/4'' \times 3'' \times 13^{1}/4''$
RR	Glass molding (Total)	$1/4'' \times 3/4'' \times 20$ ft.
SS	Lower door stiles (4)	$3/4'' \times 3'' \times 19^{3}/8''$
TT	Lower door rails (4)	$3/4'' \times 3'' \times 11^{5}/8''$
UU	Lower door panels (2)	$3/4'' \times 9^{1}/8'' \times 14^{1}/8''$
VV	Panel molding (Total)	$1/4'' \times 3/4'' \times 96''$
WW	Drawer front	$3/4'' \times 4^{5}/8'' \times 30^{5}/8''$
XX	Drawer sides (2)	$3/4'' \times 3^{7}/8'' \times 14^{3}/8''$
YY	Drawer back	$3/4'' \times 3^{7}/8'' \times 29^{1}/8''$
ZZ	Drawer bottom*	$1/4'' \times 12^{7}/8'' \times 29^{1}/8''$
AAA	Kickers (2)	$3/4'' \times 1^{1}/4'' \times 14''$

Make this part from plywood.

HARDWARE

#8 × 1¼" Flathead wood screws (26)

#8 × 1¾" Flathead wood screws (20)

#6 × ¾" Flathead wood screws, brass (24)

⅜" Offset hinges (4 pair)

Half-mortise lock

Escutcheon

Drawer pulls (2)

Door knobs with turn latches (2)

Shelf supports (12)

Shelf support rubber cushions (12)

Door elbow catch

Cabinet light with reflector (4 bulbs, 3 required)

Toggle switch (single pole, single throw)

#16 × 1" Wire nails (30–36)

#18 Wire sash cord (as needed)

Tempered glass shelves (3) $1/4'' \times 13^{5}/8'' \times 32^{1}/4''$

Door glass (2) $1/8'' \times 10^{7}/8'' \times 39^{3}/8''$

RESOURCES

Some of this hardware may be purchased from:
Paxton Hardware LTD
P.O. Box 256
Upper Falls, MD 21156

How do I build it?

PREPARING THE MATERIALS

The china cabinet shown is made from about 65 board feet of solid walnut. Old-time craftsmen who worked in the Chippendale style would have preferred mahogany, but walnut was considered a good second choice. The back is ¼-inch birch plywood. The light-colored birch brightens the interior of the cabinet.

Let the lumber dry for a few days in the shop, then bust it down. Although I usually like to bust down all my lumber at once, I suggest you don't do that for this project. There are just too many pieces to keep track of. Instead, divide it into three smaller projects: Make the case first, then the base and the top, then the doors and drawer.

MAKING THE CASE

Like the bookcase, the china cabinet case is a box with a face frame. But in this box, one of the components is a *web frame* — a frame-and-panel assembly designed to support the drawer. The web frame rests horizontally, joined to the cabinet sides like a fixed shelf.

MAKING THE CASE JOINERY The parts of the case are joined with rabbets and dadoes cut in the sides.

CONSIDER THIS!

Most commercially available walnut lumber is steamed as it's dried in the kiln. The steam partially dissolves the *extractives* — the chemicals that give wood its color — and spreads them evenly throughout the wood, making the heartwood and the sapwood roughly the same color. Although this method darkens the sapwood, it washes out the color in the heartwood, and the overall color looks bland. For that reason, I look for *air-dried* lumber when I'm making a project from walnut — there's less usable wood, but the colors are more vibrant. The drawback is that air-dried walnut may not match walnut-veneer plywood. The veneer logs are boiled before they're cut, which also washes out the color.

Rout this joinery, using a T-square router guide (page 13) to guide the router.

Drilling the Holes for Shelving Support. Both the top and the bottom of the cabinet may be filled with adjustable shelves. The shelves rest on support pins, and the pins rest in stopped holes in the sides. Drill the rows of holes with the aid of a hole-spacing guide, similar to the one shown on page 17.

In fact, you may have to make *two* guides. This is because the rows of holes in the upper portion of the case are set forward from those in the lower

ALTERNATIVES ■ *Knockdown Case Hardware*

Just in case you're wondering if there are any other ways to assemble a case besides rabbets, dadoes, and grooves, there are. Contemporary furniture designs often make use of knockdown fittings. As the term indicates, this hardware is intended to be used in pieces that must be dismantled from time to time. But many manufacturers and some craftsmen — especially craftsmen who must ship their products long distances — have begun using them for more permanent constructions as well.

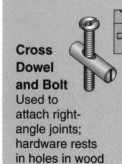

Cross Dowel and Bolt
Used to attach right-angle joints; hardware rests in holes in wood

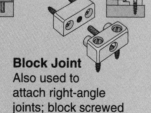

Block Joint
Also used to attach right-angle joints; block screwed to inside surfaces

Cabinet Connector
Used to join parts face to face

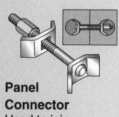

Panel Connector
Used to join panels edge to edge

Cam Connector
Used for both corner and edge joints; extremely easy to connect, just turn cam

part. The reason for this is the interior lighting. Jim installed lights in this cabinet — they are attached to the underside of the top, hidden behind baffles. If you'd like to use wooden shelves instead of the glass shelves shown, the top shelf would block the light and everything beneath it would be in shadow. But if you set the shelves forward, leaving a gap at the back, the light washes down the back of the cabinet, backlighting

Look Here! For more information on making a cabinet case, see page 10; making adjustable shelves, see page 16; wiring a cabinet, see page 98.

FRONT VIEW

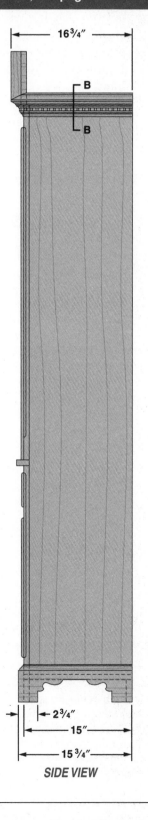

SIDE VIEW

everything on the shelves. If you don't intend to light the cabinet interior, you can align both the upper and lower sets of shelving support holes.

MAKING THE FACE FRAMES There are actually two face frames to this cabinet — top and bottom. The frames are divided at the waist (middle) by a fixed shelf or counter that overhangs the bottom frame. Each of the frames is assembled with dowel joints.

NOTCHING THE COUNTER The middle fixed shelf or counter assembly is made by

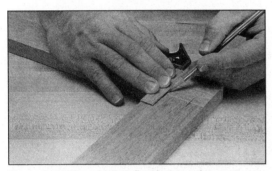

To make a dowel joint, first lay out the parts on your workbench as you want to assemble them. If necessary, clamp them together. Mark the location of the dowels, scribing each mark across the seam between the adjoining parts so *both* parts are marked.

Then, using a doweling jig to guide a portable drill, make stopped holes at each of the marks. The combined depth of each set of matching holes should be just a little more than the length of the dowels. Insert dowels in the holes and assemble the joints.

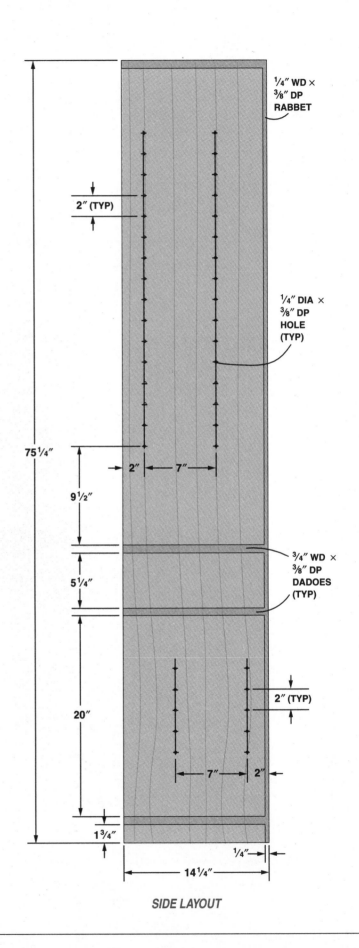

SIDE LAYOUT

¼" WD × ⅜" DP RABBET

¼" DIA × ⅜" DP HOLE (TYP)

¾" WD × ⅜" DP DADOES (TYP)

2" (TYP)

75¼"

2" (TYP)

9½"

5¼"

20"

1¾"

2" 7"

7" 2"

¼"

14¼"

gluing the counter to the counter edge, as shown in the *Counter Assembly Layout*. The edge is longer than the counter itself and fits around the front edge of the case so the ends are flush with the outside surface of the sides.

MAKING THE VENTILATION HOLES If you plan to install lighting in the cabinet, remember that lights generate heat. You have to provide some way for that heat to escape or you risk doing some damage to the cabinet and its contents.

Ventilate the space around the lights by drilling 1¼-inch-diameter holes through the top and the back, as shown in the *Top Layout-Bottom View* and the *Back Panel Layout*.

ANOTHER WAY TO GO

It's typical for classic standing cabinets such as these to have a *waist molding* dividing the upper and lower sections of the case. The middle shelf, because it protrudes from the front of the cabinet, creates the same visual effect as this molding. If you'd rather use a waist molding, eliminate the protruding portion of the shelf. Apply a ¾-inch-wide molding to the front edge of the shelf and the sides.

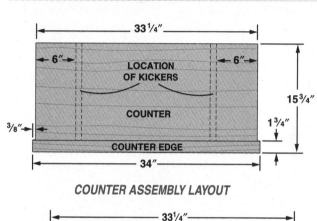

COUNTER ASSEMBLY LAYOUT

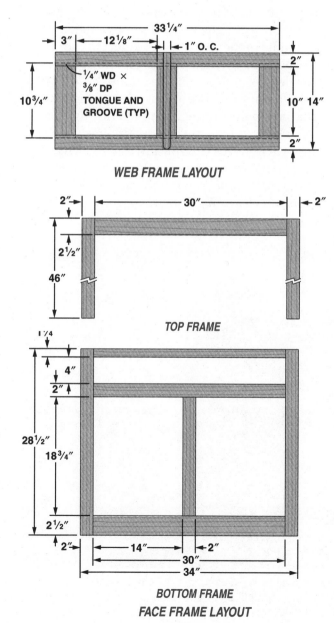

WEB FRAME LAYOUT

TOP FRAME

BOTTOM FRAME
FACE FRAME LAYOUT

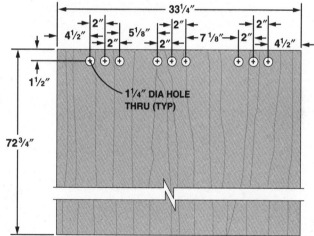

BACK PANEL LAYOUT

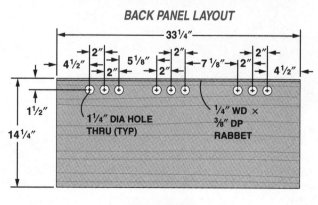

BOTTOM VIEW
TOP LAYOUT

MAKING THE WEB FRAME A web frame is a frame-and-panel assembly designed to support drawers, although I've seen web frames used for other purposes. In the entertainment center on page 78, for example, Mary Jane had our guest craftsman, Daniel Garber, use a web frame to attach the case top.

As you might expect, a typical web frame consists of rails, stiles, and panels. The frame members are grooved to hold the panels. The purpose of the panels in a web frame is to keep the dust that accumulates inside the case from settling on the contents below. Consequently, these panels are commonly called *dust shields*. Depending on the design of the cabinet and the purpose of the web frame, you may choose to omit the shields. The china cabinet's web frame does not have dust shields, but you can include them if you like.

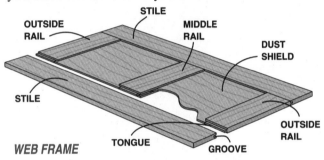

OUTSIDE RAIL

STILE

MIDDLE RAIL

DUST SHIELD

STILE

OUTSIDE RAIL

WEB FRAME   TONGUE   GROOVE

Web Frame Joinery. Usually, a web frame is joined with tongue-and-groove joints. (The tongues are sometimes called *stub tenons*.) Rout or cut grooves in the inside edges of the stiles. If the web frame will hold dust shields, make grooves in the inside edges of the rails as well. Then cut tongues in the ends of the rails to fit the grooves. When you assemble the web frame, glue the tongues in the grooves.

Guides and Kickers. Depending on your cabinet design, you may want to add *drawer guides* and *kickers* to your web frames after assembly.

A drawer guide keeps the drawer traveling in a straight line as you pull it out and push it into the case. Most craftsmen position drawer guides at the sides of the web frame to contact the drawer side. On this project, I elected to mount a single guide in the middle of the web frame, parallel to the middle rail. Then Jim notched the back of the drawer to straddle this guide, as shown on the *Drawer Back Layout* on page 76. I've also seen craftsmen attach a channel to the drawer bottom to ride the guide.

A kicker keeps a drawer from tipping when you pull it out of the case. Typically, designers use two kickers per drawer, one on either side. The kickers are attached to the web frame immediately above the drawer or to a fixed shelf.

When making a web frame, first cut the grooves in the inside edges of the rails and stiles. These grooves must be centered in the edges, so pass the boards over the cutter twice. Before the second pass, turn the boards end for end.

Cut the stub tenons in the ends of the rails by making pairs of rabbets. Cut the first rabbet in each end, then flip the board face for face and cut the second. This will center the tenons in the boards.

CONSIDER THIS!

The grain in the kickers runs perpendicular to the grain in the counter. If you glue the kickers to it, they will restrict the natural movement of the counter, potentially causing it to crack. To prevent this, screw the kickers in place, drilling holes in the kickers that are slightly larger than the screw shanks. This arrangement allows the counter to expand and contract unrestricted.

The drawer guide keeps the drawer aligned as it's pushed and pulled in and out of the case. The kickers keep it from tipping forward when it's pulled out.

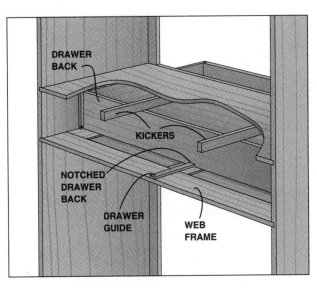

ASSEMBLING THE CASE Once you've cut the case joinery and glued up the face frames and web frame, it's time to assemble the case. There are some large parts in this project, and the case itself is a large assembly. You'll find a second pair of hands can be a real boon.

TRY THIS!

Use the Sawing Grid on page 88 as an assembly table while putting the case together. A typical workbench is too high for assembling large projects comfortably.

Assemble the sides, fixed shelves, and counter with glue. Attach the web frame with screws, as shown in the photo below but now with glue. Then glue the face frames to the front edges of the sides and shelves. Finally, attach the back with brads. You can glue the back in place if you want, but most craftsmen choose not to. Attaching the back with small nails makes it easier to remove should you ever need to repair the case.

After the case is assembled and the glue is dry, profile the front arrises by cutting a chamfer with a router. Note that this chamfer is stopped, as shown in the *Front View* on page 59. It doesn't continue all the way up and down the case.

When assembling the web frame to the sides, drive the screws at an angle up through the web frame and into the sides. *Don't* glue these parts together. The screws allow the sides and the frame members to move independently.

After assembling the case, cut stopped chamfers in the front arrises with a router and a chamfering bit. The top ends of the chamfers should be even with the tops of the doors or drawers on the completed cabinet. The bottom ends of the top chamfers should be even with the top edges of the glazed door rails. The bottom ends of the bottom chamfers should be even with the bottom edges of the paneled doors.

MAKING A FRAME BASE

A frame base supports the case on a simple frame. Typically, the front and side faces of the frame stand out from the front of the case, while the back surfaces are flush — the *Side View* on page 59 shows you what I mean. The front corners of the frame are mitered; the back corners are butted. All four corners are reinforced with glue blocks.

I strongly suggest you *don't* cut the parts for the base until after you've assembled the case. No matter how exacting a craftsman you are, the case always turns out slightly larger or smaller than your plans. At least, it does for both Jim and me. So we cut assemblies like a frame base to fit the completed case.

CUTTING THE PARTS To make the frame base, rip the base molding to width and shape the top edge.

Cut the front and the side moldings, mitering the adjoining corners. Cut the sides a little long. Temporarily assemble the parts with miter clamps or Corner Squares (page 75). Slip the assembly over the bottom end of the case to make sure it fits. When you are satisfied that it does, mark the back ends of the side base moldings and cut them to length. Also cut the base back, corner blocks, and ledges.

Once the parts are cut and fit, cut the profiles of the feet. Photocopy the full-size *Foot Pattern* and *Base Center Ornament Pattern* on the facing page or design your own. Cut the profiles with a band saw or a saber saw, then sand the edges smooth.

ASSEMBLING THE BASE Assemble the base with glue and screws. Screw the cleats to the base frame first, then to the sides and bottom of the case, as shown in the *Base Joinery Detail* on the facing page.

Jim left the base and the pediment unattached until it was time to apply a finish to the cabinet. He found it easier to finish-sand individual subassemblies than it would have been to sand the assembled cabinet.

Cut an ogee shape in the top edge of the base molding using a router or a shaper.

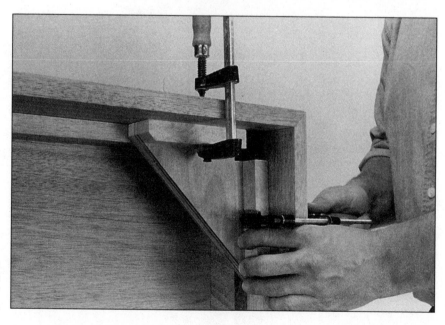

To fit the frame base to the case, temporarily assemble the frame members by clamping them together with corner squares.

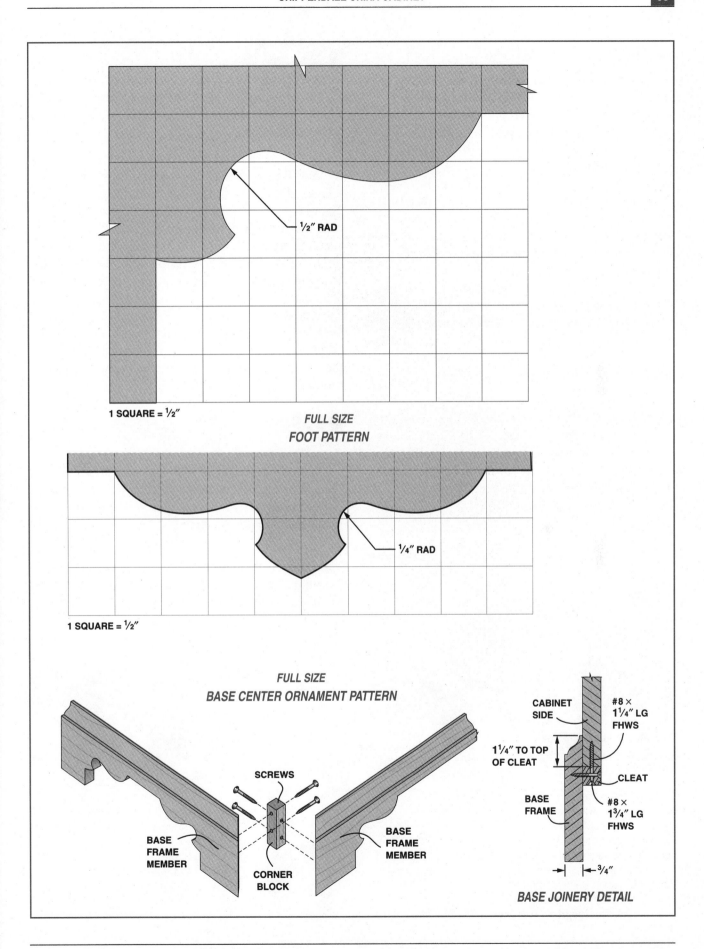

1 SQUARE = 1/2"

1/2" RAD

FULL SIZE
FOOT PATTERN

1/4" RAD

1 SQUARE = 1/2"

FULL SIZE
BASE CENTER ORNAMENT PATTERN

SCREWS

BASE
FRAME
MEMBER

CORNER
BLOCK

BASE
FRAME
MEMBER

CABINET
SIDE

#8 ×
1 1/4" LG
FHWS

1 1/4" TO TOP
OF CLEAT

CLEAT

BASE
FRAME

#8 ×
1 3/4" LG
FHWS

3/4"

BASE JOINERY DETAIL

MAKING A PEDIMENT TOP

Old-time cabinetmakers modeled "pediment" tops after the roof lines of ancient Greek and Roman temples. The top that Jim built is actually a "broken pediment," so called because the two halves of the roof are separated by a circular cutout.

It looks difficult to make, and I have to be honest with you, it's not a cakewalk. Like any complex woodworking project, however, it can be broken down into a series of simple steps. The intricate molded shapes are built up in several easy-to-make layers. The trim around the top of the pediment consists of an ogee, a bead, a cove, and a rectangular "dentil" molding, as shown in *Section A* on the facing page. The trim around the bottom is made up of a small bead and cove. Despite the angle of the pediment, you don't have to cut odd angles to fit the moldings. With one exception, all of the trim parts are joined with ordinary 45-degree miters.

MAKING THE MOLDING The first step is to create the molded shapes. Plane boards to the thickness needed for each shape. Rout the shape in the edge of a wide board, them rip the shaped edge from it.

To make the dentil molding, cut a series of evenly spaced dadoes in the stock. Note that the

SAFEGUARD

Never shape the edges of thin strips. This brings your fingers much too close to the whirling cutters. Furthermore, the fragile strips may break as you shape them.

dadoes in the side moldings are square to the edges, while those in the front moldings are angled 70 degrees to the edges — this angle is the reciprocal of the pediment slope angle. (To find the *reciprocal* of an angle, subtract the angle from 90 degrees.) When installed, both sets of dadoes run straight up and down. After cutting the dadoes, rip the boards into strips. Note that the top edges of the side dentil moldings are beveled at 20 degrees, as shown in *Section B* on the facing page, and *both* edges in the "return" dentil moldings (the pieces inside the arc) are beveled, as shown in the *Return Molding Detail* on the facing page.

CONSIDER THIS!

Cut more molding than you think you'll need — Jim found this out the hard way. He cut just as much as he thought he'd need, then cut a piece too short. Jim had to backtrack and rout a whole new set of molded shapes.

Lay up the trim by gluing the strips face to face. Laminate the large ogee, bead, and cove to make the top trim, and the small bead and cove to make the bottom trim. Don't glue up the dentil molding yet.

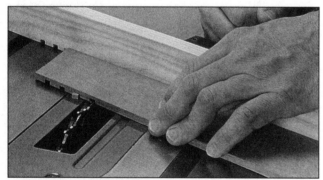

Lay up the molded strips, gluing them face to face, as shown in *Section A*. When the moldings are assembled, you should have three strips — the top trim, dentil molding, and bottom trim. **Note: Masking tape makes a good "clamp" for these gluing operations.**

To make the dentil molding, saw evenly spaced ¼-inch-wide, ¼-inch-deep dadoes in a board every ½ inch. To help space the dadoes, make the dado spacing guide *(shown)* and attach it to your miter gauge. Cut a dado, move the stock sideways until the dado fits over the finger, and repeat. To make the angled dadoes, set the miter gauge at a 70 degree angle.

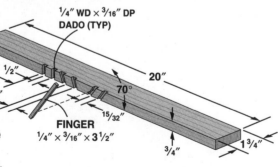

¼" WD × ³⁄₁₆" DP DADO (TYP)

5½"   ½"

15/32

FINGER
¼" × ³⁄₁₆" × 3½"

20"

70°

15/32

¾"

1¾"

DADO SPACING GUIDE

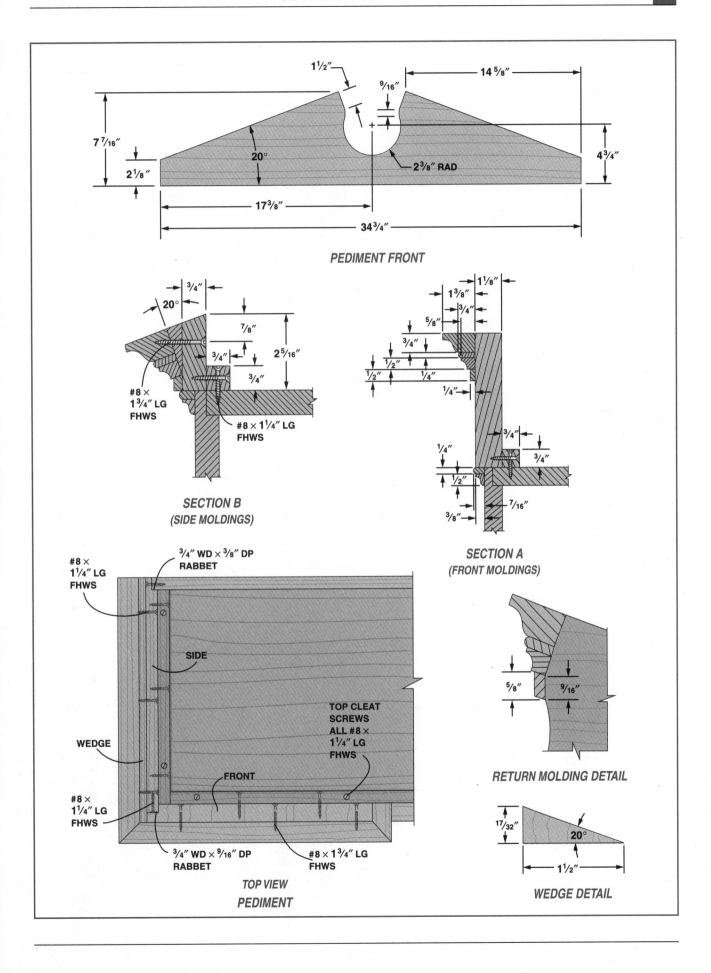

PEDIMENT FRONT

SECTION B
(SIDE MOLDINGS)

SECTION A
(FRONT MOLDINGS)

RETURN MOLDING DETAIL

WEDGE DETAIL

TOP VIEW
PEDIMENT

ASSEMBLING THE TOP Measure the top of the case so you know its true dimensions, then cut the pediment front, sides, and back to fit. Note that the top edges of the sides are beveled at 20 degrees, as shown in *Section B* on page 67.

Cut rabbets in the ends of the pediment front and the rear ends of the sides, as shown in the *Pediment–Top View* on page 67. Also cut cleats to fit inside the pediment frame on the sides and front, and saw the profile of the front, as shown in the *Pediment Front* on page 67. Assemble the pediment parts with glue and screws.

FITTING THE TRIM Now comes a neat trick. When Jim and I first looked at Mary Jane's design for the pediment, we wondered how we'd ever calculate the angles we needed to cut to join the side and front trim. Then Jim came up with a solution that sidesteps the problem — glue a 20-degree wedge to the outside faces of the sides (as shown in *Section B*). With the wedges in place, you can make all the miters at 45 degrees.

Rest the pediment on your workbench — Jim found it a lot easier to fit most of the remaining trim this way. Attach the top trim, mitering the strips to turn the outside corners and the corners at the peak, where the pediment is broken. As you fit each piece, attach it temporarily with carpet tape. When you're certain all the parts fit, go back and fasten them with glue and screws.

Next, secure the dentil molding. Remember, use the strips with the beveled top edges on the sides,

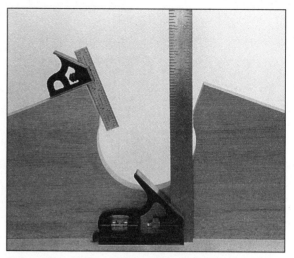

The profile of the pediment front requires careful layout. The two ⁹⁄₁₆-inch-wide flats on either side of the arc must be precisely square to the bottom edge. And the 1½-inch-wide flats just above them must be 20 degrees from the smaller flats and square to the top edges.

and those with both edges beveled inside the arc. Cut simple 45-degree miters in the parts with one or two beveled edges, but you must compound-miter the other parts — the front dentil moldings.

Finally, attach the pediment assembly to the top of the case with screws. Miter the bottom trim, and glue it to the bottom edge of the pediment front and sides. Try not to get any glue on the case. You want to be able to remove the pediment to sand and finish it.

The only trim parts that require compound miters are the front dentil moldings. When you cut their ends, set the blade tilt to 45 degrees and the miter gauge to 20 degrees.

ALTERNATIVES ■ *Crown Molding — A Simpler Top*

If you don't feel up to making the pediment top, well, I don't blame you. It takes some experience to work up to something like that. Jim admitted it was a stretch for him, and he's a master craftsman.

I built a piece very similar to this cabinet years ago, but I trimmed the top with a simple *bed molding* — a large cove and a smaller bead *(see photo at right)*. You can make the bead with a router or a shaper, but you must cut the cove on a table saw as explained here.

1 Attach a straightedge to the work surface of your table saw at a 30-degree angle to the blade, as shown. You can clamp the straightedge at the ends or hold it down with double-faced carpet tape.

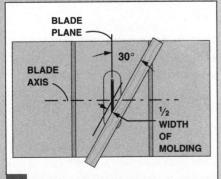

2 Cut a strip of wood ¾ inch thick and 2⅝ inches wide. Lower the saw blade so it protrudes just ¹⁄₁₆ inch above the work surface. Pass the wood over the blade slowly, keeping it firmly against the angled straightedge. The blade should cut a shallow cove down the middle of the board. Raise the saw another ¹⁄₁₆ inch and make another pass. Repeat until you have cut a cove that's ½ inch deep.

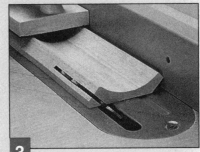

3 Bevel-rip the edges of the cove molding with the saw blade set at 45 degrees, as shown.

4 Glue the cove molding to the bead molding so the cove leans out at 45 degrees. (This is called a *sprung molding.*) Reinforce the sprung molding with triangular glue block every 6 inches or so, as shown in the drawing. Miter the trim and attach the part to the case with screws, driving the screws from *inside* the case so they won't be seen. *Don't glue the molding to the sides!* Remember, the grain direction of the molding runs perpendicular to the sides. If you glue the two parts together, the molding will restrict the wood movement and the sides will warp. Instead, use screws only. Drill oversized holes for the screw shanks in the case so the sides can expand and contract freely.

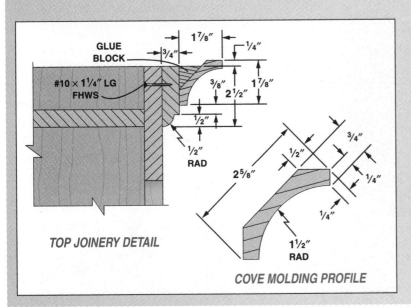

TOP JOINERY DETAIL

COVE MOLDING PROFILE

MAKING AND HANGING THE DOORS

There are two sets of doors on this cabinet, as I mentioned earlier. Both sets are lipped; that is, the edges are rabbeted so the frame fits inside the door opening but the lips cover the opening. For this reason, the doors require offset hinges.

The bottom doors are frame-and-panel assemblies with raised panels — similar to the door on the spice cupboard (page 2). The top doors are glazed, similar to those on the mission bookcase (page 30).

But there are some interesting differences. First of all, the top doors are double doors. The inside stiles are rabbeted so the right door laps over the left by ⁵⁄₁₆ inch, as shown in the *Top Door Section* on the facing page.

Second, the top rail in each door is arched to give it more visual interest. Note that the glass rabbet, however, is rectangular, as shown in the *Top Door Layout* on the facing page. I made the doors this way so I could purchase ordinary panes of glass for the doors. If I had cut a uniform rabbet to follow the arch on the top rails, I would need a glass store to make special arched panels to fit. You can do this if you want, but I elected to save a little money.

TENONS — TO SPLIT OR NOT TO SPLIT Finally, the top rails have *split tenons.* Instead of making a

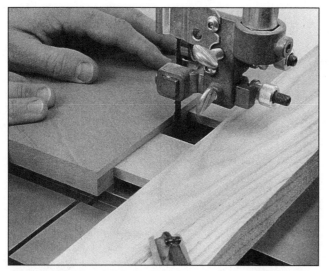

When cutting away the waste between split tenons, cut the bottom of the notch perfectly flat by "nibbling" the surface with a band saw blade. Attach a fence behind the blade and perpendicular to its side. Guide the wood along the fence, letting the sides of the saw teeth cut the wood like a rasp.

single 6-inch-wide tenon on each end, I elected to make two narrower tenons. The reason I did this is two-fold. First, long mortises weaken the stiles. Second, the wood grain in the cheeks of a tenon is perpendicular to the sides of the mortise. The two pieces of wood expand and contract in opposite directions. This is tolerable for small surfaces — the rule of thumb is that it's okay for any glued surface less than 3 inches across the grain. But larger assemblies may warp, buckle, and split. So I made the tenons just 2 inches wide, like those on the other rails.

Understand that this was by no means a clearcut decision. Many craftsmen maintain that splitting a tenon is unnecessary work; it makes no difference. The entire rail is going to move across its 7-inch width, stressing the joint no matter how many tenons there are. This is true; I can't deny it. But I also believe that splitting a wide tenon relieves some of that stress and extends the life of the joint.

MAKING THE DOOR JOINERY Both sets of doors are assembled with blind mortises and tenons — the mortises don't go all the way through the stiles. When the door frames are assembled, the joints are *blind* — you can't see them. However, they are made in exactly the same way as the mortise-and-tenon joints in the mission bookcase (page 30). Stop cutting the mortises when they are 1½ inches deep.

Look Here! For more information on making a frame-and-panel door, see page 20, or making glazed doors, see page 40.

CUTTING THE ARCHES Lay out the arches on the bottom edges of the top door rails. Cut the arches with a band saw or saber saw, then sand them smooth.

TRY THIS!

You can save yourself a little time by pad sawing the arches. Stack the parts face to face, holding them together with double-faced carpet tape. Mark an arc on the top board, then saw through both boards at once.

ASSEMBLING THE DOORS Assemble the door frames and let the glue dry. Then rabbet both the inside and outside edges, as shown in the *Door Panel Joinery Detail*. The outside rabbets create the lips, while the inside rabbets hold the glass or the raised panels. Ordinarily, you'd make a frame-and-panel door with grooves to hold the panel. I elected to cut rabbets in both sets of doors just to keep the construction simpler. There aren't as many setups.

I raised the panels with a vertical panel-raising bit, cutting shallow coves in the ends and edges. To keep the wooden panels in the rabbets, I screwed narrow moldings to the inside surfaces of the door frame straddling the seam between the panel and the frame.

You might be thinking that these inside moldings created more work than they saved — and you may be right. But I had another reason for using this construction. By setting the panels in a rabbet, I could make the panel thicker and the cove around the edges deeper. This, in turn, enhanced the visual effect of the raised panels.

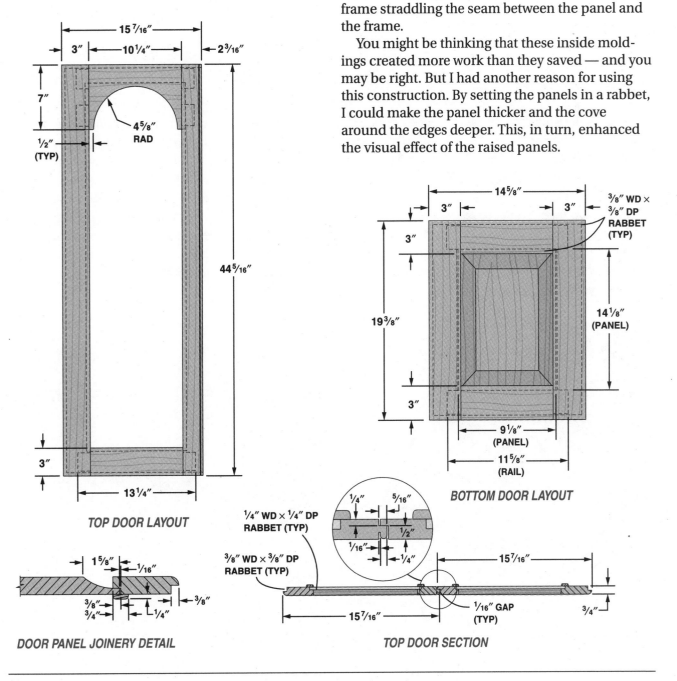

TOP DOOR LAYOUT

BOTTOM DOOR LAYOUT

DOOR PANEL JOINERY DETAIL

TOP DOOR SECTION

HANGING THE DOORS One of the advantages of lipped doors is that they are simple to hang. There are no exacting measurements to make, no mortises to cut. However, you must do things in the proper order.

■ Attach the offset leaves of the hinges to the door stiles, each hinge the same distance from the nearest end of the stile. Make sure the bend in the leaves follows the lips.

■ Position the doors on the case. You want there to be a slight gap between the face frame and the shoulders of the lip rabbet. I do this by feel. I place the door on the case, slide it around so I know where it stops when the shoulders bump against

TRY THIS!

You can adjust offset hinges by bending or "springing" them ever so slightly. If the doors don't align or the top or bottom shoulders of a lip rub on the door opening, pull the door up or down to spring a hinge. Be very gentle when you do this; it doesn't take much pressure.

the frame, then position it somewhere in the middle.

■ Once the door is in position, mark and drill the pilot hole for the face frame leaves. Then screw the hinges to the face frame.

NO PROBLEM ■ *Correcting Warped Doors and Face Frames*

You select the straightest wood you can find for the rails and stiles, assemble the doors as carefully as you can so they are square and flat, then mount them on the case and — what the heck! They won't lie flat against the face frame when they are closed. Unless you push really hard,

one corner seems to stand out from the case. No problem. You can fix this either by resetting the hinges or by planing the mating surfaces.

First, identify the culprit. Are the hinges properly aligned? If not, move one of them into alignment with the other. Plug the screw holes with toothpicks or

match sticks, then reattach the hinge to the case.

If the hinges are set properly, check the straightness and flatness of the assemblies. Are the door rails or stiles bowed? Is the face frame warped? What part do you need to make straight and true?

1   Once you've found the offending part, plane the inside surface of the lip with a rabbet plane to fit the door to the face frame.

2   Or, plane the face frame to fit it to the door frame, using a hand plane or a block plane. In all probability you'll have to plane both the inside surface and the face frame. Remove a little stock, check your work, then remove a little more until the door fits properly. Afterwards, blend the surfaces so there are no noticeable high spots or dips.

MAKING AND HANGING THE DRAWER

A drawer is just a box, open at the top. In fact, drawers were once called "drawing boxes" — boxes that you pull or draw out of the case.

As with any box, there are a couple zillion joints you can use to join the corners. Most drawers are assembled with three different joints. At the back corners, where the stress is least, the back fits into a simple dado or rabbet in the sides. At the front corners, where the stress is greatest, the corners are joined with dovetails, lock joints, or some other more durable joint. And the bottom floats in grooves cut in the inside faces of the front, back, and sides.

MAKING THE DRAWER JOINERY The only joints on this list that we haven't covered earlier are those at the front corners. Half-blind dovetails are the traditional choice of most craftsmen, but they can be time-consuming to make, even if you have a special dovetail template that enables you to rout them. I prefer lock joints. They're almost as strong, and the setups needed to make them are far simpler.

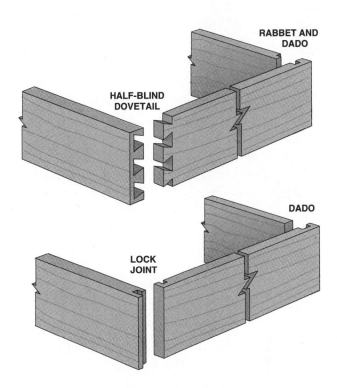

DRAWER JOINERY OPTIONS

QUICK FIXTURE ■ *Lock Joint Jig*

The lock joint jig is an MDF spacer that rests on the work surface of your table saw. This reduces the depth of cut when cutting the short tenon and the dado in a lock joint. The thickness of the spacer should be exactly two-thirds the thickness of the drawer stock. If you're using ¾-inch stock, make the jig from ½-inch MDF. For ⅜-inch-thick stock, use ¼-inch MDF.

To secure the spacer on the table saw, attach it to the work surface with double-faced carpet tape. Most MDF is slightly thinner than its nominal thickness. The carpet tape not only secures the spacer; it helps make up this difference. See page 74 for instructions on how to use this jig.

Note: When making *lipped* drawers (as on the china cabinet), you will need an additional spacer.

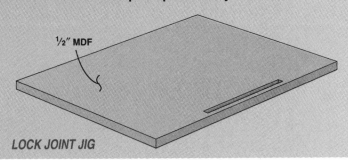

LOCK JOINT JIG

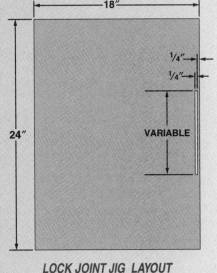

LOCK JOINT JIG LAYOUT

METHODS OF WORK ▪ *Making a Lock Joint*

A lock joint is an interlocking tongue, groove, and dado, joined so the joint is half-blind. You can see it at the side and top of the drawer but not at the front.

You can make a lock joint with a single setup, using a lock joint jig as a spacer on your table saw. However, the width and thickness of the tongues, grooves, and dadoes must all be equal to one-third of the thickness of the stock. If you're working with ¾-inch-thick stock, for example, they should all be ¼ inch wide or thick. If the dimensions differ, you won't be able to use the jig, and you'll have to make three setups.

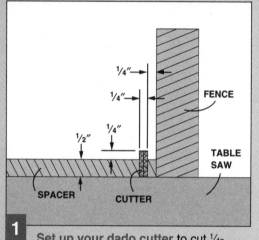

1 Set up your dado cutter to cut ¼-inch-wide, ¾-inch-deep grooves, and position the fence ¼ inch away from the cutter.

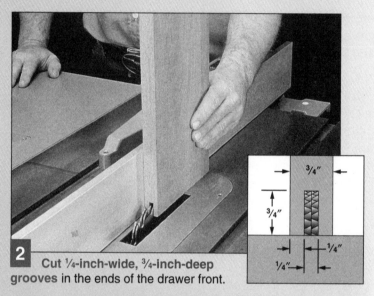

2 Cut ¼-inch-wide, ¾-inch-deep grooves in the ends of the drawer front.

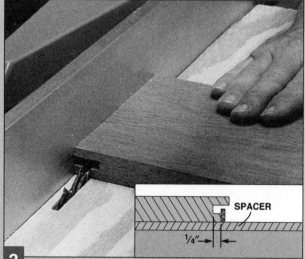

3 The grooves create two tenons at each end of the drawer front. Place the lock joint jig on the work surface of the table saw and cut the *inside* tenons ¼ inch long. **Warning: Use a thick scrap to back up the cut and help feed the stock. This will reduce the chances of a kickback and keep the stock square to the blade.**

4 With the jig still in place, cut ¼-inch-wide, ¼-inch-deep grooves near the front ends of the sides.

After you cut the lock joints, dadoes, and grooves that hold the drawer together, cut a ⅛-inch-deep, 1⅛-inch-wide notch in the bottom edge of the drawer back, as shown in the *Drawer Back Layout* on page 76. As I explained earlier, this notch fits over the drawer guide on the web frame.

ASSEMBLING THE DRAWER Assemble the drawer front, back, and sides with glue. As you join them, slide the bottom into its grooves. Don't glue it in place; let it float.

It's very important that the drawer go together square and flat. To keep the corners square, use miter clamps to hold the drawer parts while the glue dries. Or you can clamp corner squares at the corners. These also keep the corners aligned.

After the glue dries on the front, back, and sides, attach the drawer face to the drawer front. The face must overlap the front an equal amount on all four sides. Also install drawer pulls. Then slide the drawer into the case.

CONSIDER THIS!

In this project, I made the drawer bottom from plywood. Since plywood is relatively stable, I wasn't overly concerned with wood movement. I simply cut the plywood a little (about 1/16 inch) smaller than the grooves. However, if you make the bottom from solid wood, you need to give the matter a little thought. Arrange the wood grain in the bottom so it runs side to side (parallel to the front and back). Cut the bottom about ¼ inch undersized across the grain. If the grain were parallel to the sides, the bottom would expand and contract too much. You'd have to cut the bottom over ½ inch short to allow for all that movement, and there would be a gap at one side of the drawer during the dry part of the year.

QUICK FIXTURE ■ *Corner Square*

A corner square holds two parts 90 degrees to one another. Each square is a right triangle made from a scrap of plywood. I've attached two cleats to each triangle, flush with the sides. This lets you attach the corner squares with small clamps. The notch in the corner helps prevent the squeezed-out glue in the corners from sticking the square to the project.

Make four squares. On large projects, you may need them all. On most small projects, like this drawer, I've found that you need only two placed diagonally to one another.

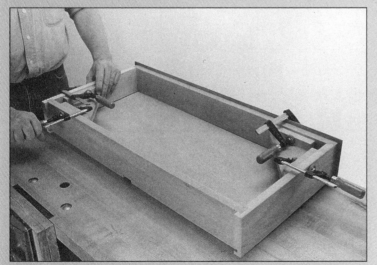

Attach the corner squares to the project with small clamps. Be sure to place cauls between the workpiece and the clamp jaws to prevent the jaws from leaving dents in the wood.

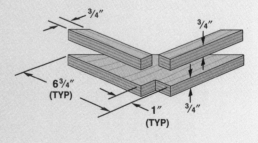

EXPLODED VIEW
CORNER SQUARE

FINISHING THE CABINET

Once you have made the various parts of the cabinet, remove the pediment top, frame base, doors, and drawer. Also remove the hardware and set it aside. Do any finish-sanding you need to do, then apply a finish. For this project, Jim applied a hand-rubbed tung oil finish. However, that's only a suggestion. Almost any clear finish will work well.

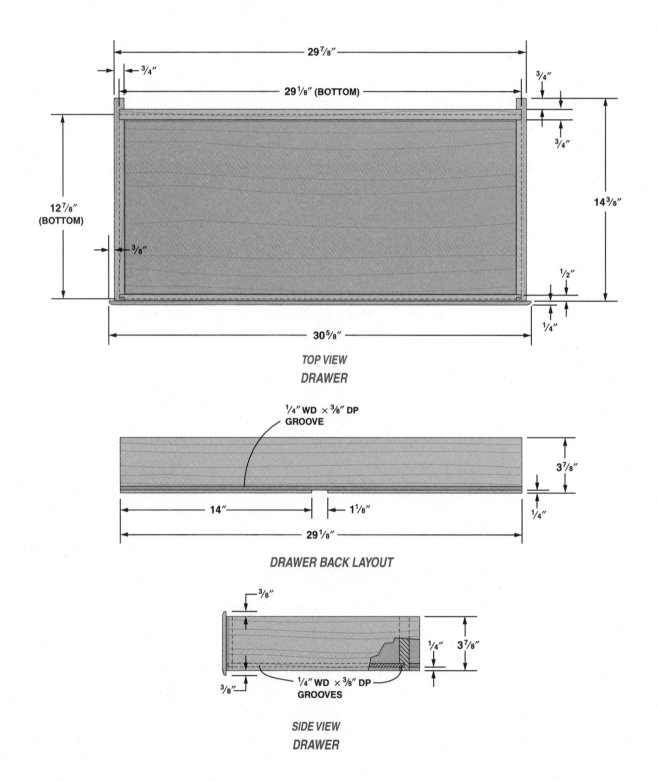

TOP VIEW
DRAWER

DRAWER BACK LAYOUT

SIDE VIEW
DRAWER

ALTERNATIVES ▪ *Common Methods of Hanging Drawers*

The web frame is one of the oldest ways to hang a drawer. However, it is by no means the only way. Here are three good alternatives:

Drawer Guides. These are best suited for small and light-duty drawers. Mount horizontal strips of wood in the sides of the case to support and guide the drawer. Then cut grooves in the drawer sides to fit over the guide strips. There should be a little play in the drawers — the guides must not be snug in the grooves, or the drawer will bind as you pull it in and out of the case.

DRAWER GUIDE

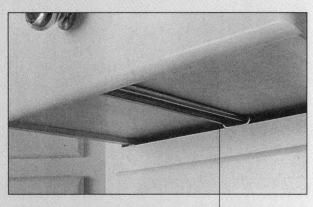

Bottom-Mounted Guides. These are for medium-duty drawers and are often used on built-in cabinets. The guide spans the depth of the cabinet at the bottom of the drawer opening. Ordinarily, you must attach one end to the inside surface of the face frame and the other to the cabinet back or nailing strip. Screw a roller to the back of the drawer. To mount the drawer, slide the roller into the guide.

BOTTOM-MOUNTED DRAWER GUIDE

Side-Mounted Extension Slides. These are best for drawers that will likely see heavy duty, and they'll make the contents at the back of the drawer easier to reach. Like drawer guides, extension slides support and guide the drawer from the sides. However, they don't rest in grooves. You must make the drawer 1 inch narrower (½ inch to a side) than the drawer opening to make room for this hardware. Screw the slides to the inside of the case, and attach the mounting brackets to the drawer sides. Snap the brackets into the slide, and you're in business.

Look Here! For more information on extension slides, see pages 95–96.

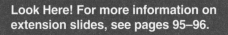

SIDE-MOUNTED EXTENSION SLIDE

Entertainment Center

This entertainment center, made by craftsman Daniel Garber, looks like an old-time wardrobe or linen press, but it opens up to reveal audio and video equipment. The drawers are sized to serve as files for videotapes.

Actually, this cabinet is made in a similar manner to a linen press. There's nothing special about the case, the doors, or the drawers other than that they are sized to hold electronics and tapes instead of sheets and pillowcases. They are assembled with ordinary joints, made with ordinary methods.

There are some subtle differences, however. Most important, the cabinet is *ventilated*. It has openings in various locations that encourage air flow through the interior and help keep the electronic components cool. It's also wired to provide power to the equipment and protect it from power surges. The doors are mounted on special hardware that allows them to open and slide back into the cabinet. This prevents them from blocking anyone's view of the television. Finally, the drawers are mounted on hardware that lets you slide them all the way out of the case, like file drawers. This, in turn, makes it easier to reach the tapes in the back of the drawers.

What size should it be?

As always, that depends on what you want to put in it. What electronic equipment do you have? And just as important, what do you plan to buy in the near future? In addition to holding what you have, your cabinet design should be versatile enough to hold what you'd like to have, should you want to swap your old stuff for new stuff.

Fortunately, the electronics industry has provided a little help in this respect. Many of the electronic components that make up a sound or television system are built in relatively standard sizes.

SOUND COMPONENTS Probably the most standardized are sound components. Amplifiers, tuners, tape players, CD changers, and mixers will usually fit in the same *footprint*. That is, they are generally 18 inches wide and 12 inches deep. The height, however, is more widely varied. Most sound equipment is between 3½ and 5 inches tall, but individual pieces may be taller or shorter.

The wrinkle in this conformity are the mini-systems, so-called bookshelf sound systems that often include an amplifier, tuner, tape player, CD changer, and even a mixer, arranged vertically in a small "tower." Many of these towers are too tall to fit between the average bookshelves, so you'd need to build something special to hold it. Fortunately you've had the foresight to buy this book, so you have a leg up on the problem.

Most high-end sound components have the same footprint, making them easy to stack. Mini-systems, however, are not as standardized.

Sound systems also include headsets, remotes, cables, tapes, discs, and other accessories. These should have a place in a well-designed entertainment center.

VIDEO EQUIPMENT At the other end of the spectrum, there are televisions and videocassette recorders. Until very recently, VCRs were sized similarly to audio equipment, with a footprint of 12 inches × 18 inches. But that has begun to change. Digital video disc players add another dimension — it's possible to make these as small as portable CD players.

The size of a television depends on the screen size. The larger the screen, the wider, deeper, and taller the equipment. If you exclude portable televisions (which aren't stored in a cabinet) and widescreen TVs (which usually come with their own cabinet), televisions with screens between 19 and 27 inches (measured diagonally) have a depth of between 16 and 24 inches. The width and height are more varied; they depend on the position of the controls. However, they are often very close

to the depth. In short, most TVs fit in a roughly cubic space.

ACCESSORIES In addition to planning space for major electronic components, give some thought to smaller accessories. If you're building a cabinet to store a sound system, what about headphones, tapes, and CDs? Will the speakers be located outside or inside the cabinet?

If you're making a cabinet for video equipment, do your kids have gear for electronic games — controllers, joysticks, keyboards, cartridges, and so on? Do you want to store videotapes or discs? A camcorder? And where will you keep the remote when you're not using it?

AIRFLOW AND WIRING Consider the airflow around the components. We'll talk more about this on page 97, but you need to give it careful thought

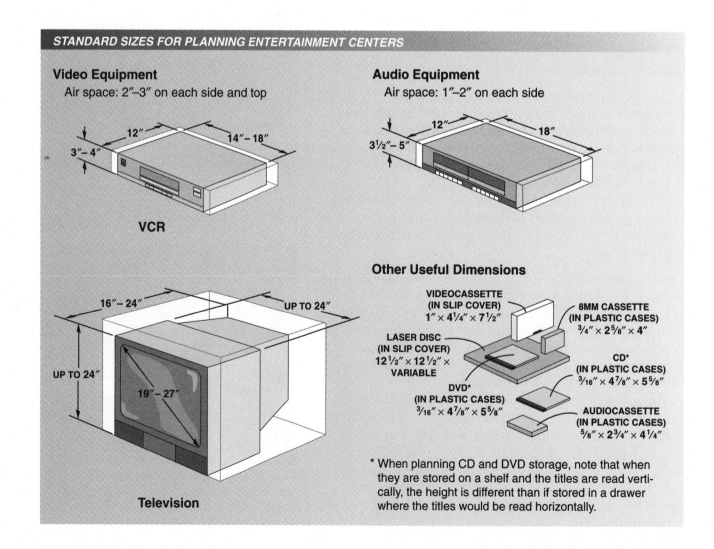

STANDARD SIZES FOR PLANNING ENTERTAINMENT CENTERS

Video Equipment
Air space: 2″–3″ on each side and top

12″ 14″–18″ 3″–4″

VCR

Audio Equipment
Air space: 1″–2″ on each side

12″ 18″ 3½″–5″

Television

16″–24″ UP TO 24″ UP TO 24″ 19″–27″

Other Useful Dimensions

VIDEOCASSETTE
(IN SLIP COVER)
1″ × 4¼″ × 7½″

8MM CASSETTE
(IN PLASTIC CASES)
¾″ × 2⅝″ × 4″

LASER DISC
(IN SLIP COVER)
12½″ × 12½″ ×
VARIABLE

CD*
(IN PLASTIC CASES)
³/₁₆″ × 4⅞″ × 5⅝″

DVD*
(IN PLASTIC CASES)
³/₁₆″ × 4⅞″ × 5⅝″

AUDIOCASSETTE
(IN PLASTIC CASES)
⅝″ × 2¾″ × 4¼″

* When planning CD and DVD storage, note that when they are stored on a shelf and the titles are read vertically, the height is different than if stored in a drawer where the titles would be read horizontally.

as you're planning the cabinet. Many electronic components require air space *around* them to provide proper ventilation and cooling. You can't pack them in the cabinet like sardines — check your manuals for airspace requirements. Finally, it's always a good idea to allow some extra space at the back of the case for wiring.

Most VCRs are about the same size as a sound component and can be included in your audio stack.

Got kids? Remember to make a space — a lot of space — for electronic gaming gear.

ALTERNATIVES ■ *Entertainment Center Hardware*

There are several types of hardware that are made especially for entertainment centers. See "Resources" on page 85.

There are many types of plastic and metal organizers *(1)* for cassettes and discs of all sizes. These can be mounted in drawers, on shelves, even to the backs of cabinet doors.

Lazy Susans *(2)* let you swivel televisions and large speakers for better viewing and listening.

TV pullouts *(3)* are combination of slides and swivels that let you pull a television partway out of a cabinet, then turn it to face one way or the other.

What style will it be?

Mary Jane designed the entertainment center in this chapter after a Shaker linen press. Shakers strived to make their furniture as functional as possible, devoid of almost all ornament. Consequently, the entertainment center has simple, straight lines. In fact, the only deviation from vertical and horizontal are the tapered feet.

The Shakers weren't bereft of design savvy, however. Much of their furniture has a strong sense of proportion. For that reason, Mary Jane made the front profile of this piece a *golden rectangle*. Here are some other possibilities.

Look Here! For more information on proportion, see page 6.

PENNSYLVANIA GERMAN STYLE

Early in the eighteenth century, German and Swiss immigrants to America banded together in tight enclaves outside of Philadelphia, where they carefully preserved their own traditions. Among these traditions were the furniture styles they brought from the Old World. This entertainment center is patterned after an old German *Schrank,* or wardrobe.

VICTORIAN OAK STYLE

Victorian homes were woefully short of closet space, so the occupants made their own with large oak cupboards similar to this one. This cupboard has been converted to hold audio and video equipment.

CONTEMPORARY STYLE

Like the Shakers a century before, Contemporary designers strive to make functional pieces whose only ornament is pleasing proportions. This Contemporary cabinet sports paneled doors and rich wood grain.

Crafted by Randal Patterson, Cheyney, PA; photo by Rick Echelmeyer

Crafted by Michael Cabaniss, Albion, CA; photo by Tony Grant

SOUTHWEST STYLE

Just as the Victorians built huge oak wardrobes to provide the storage space they lacked in their homes, Spanish settlers in the Southwest built *trasteros,* brightly colored ventilated cabinets. This audio cabinet is a Southwest *revival* piece. It borrows elements of traditional Southwest designs *(see page 7)* and mixes them with modern materials.

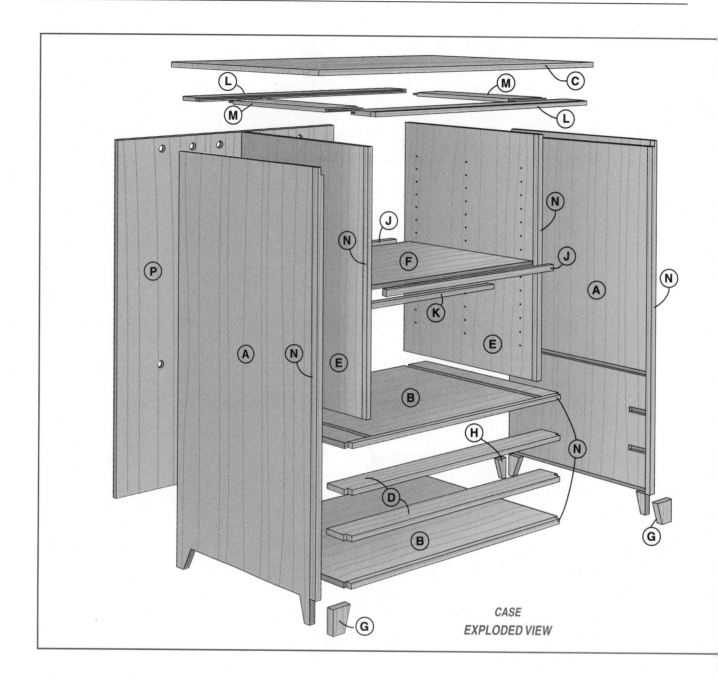

CASE
EXPLODED VIEW

ENTERTAINMENT CENTER ■ *MATERIALS LIST*

PARTS

A	Sides* (2)	¾″ × 20¾″ × 59¼″	**H**	Back feet (2)	¾″ × 1½″ × 3½″
B	Fixed shelves* (2)	¾″ × 19¾″ × 34¼″	**J**	Adjustable shelf edges (2)	¾″ × 1½″ × 27⅞″
C	Top	¾″ × 22¼″ × 36½″	**K**	Adjustable shelf ribs (2)	¾″ × ¾″ × 27⅞″
D	Drawer dividers (2)	¾″ × 3″ × 34¼″	**L**	Top frame front/back (2)	¾″ × 3″ × 34¼″
E	Vertical partitions* (2)	¾″ × 19¾″ × 34¾″	**M**	Top frame sides (2)	¾″ × 4″ × 16″
F	Adjustable shelf*	¾″ × 18″ × 27⅞″	**N**	Edging (total)	¾″ × ¾″ × 25 ft.
G	Front feet (2)	¾″ × 2¼″ × 3½″	**P**	Back*	¼″ × 34¼″ × 55¾″

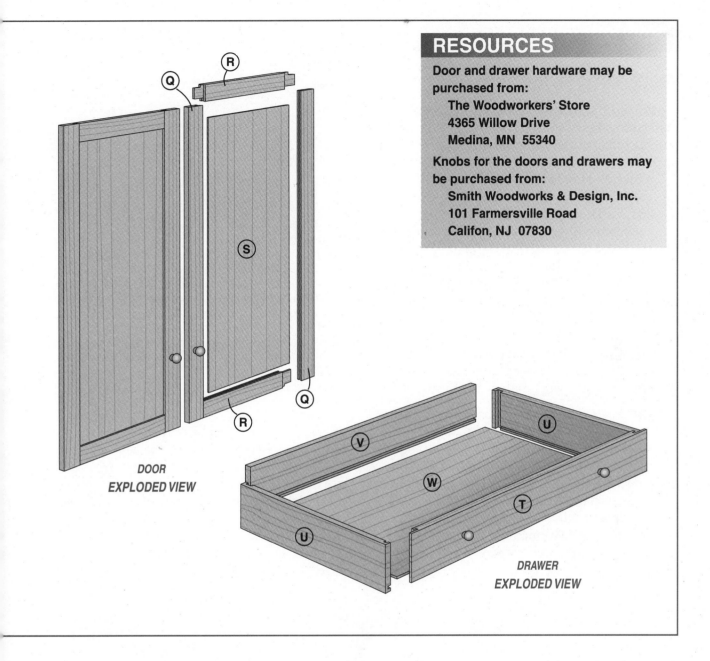

DOOR EXPLODED VIEW

DRAWER EXPLODED VIEW

Q	Door stiles (4)	$\frac{3}{4}'' \times 2'' \times 34''$
R	Door rails (4)	$\frac{3}{4}'' \times 2'' \times 15\frac{3}{4}''$
S	Door panels* (2)	$\frac{1}{4}'' \times 13\frac{1}{2}'' \times 30\frac{3}{4}''$
T	Drawer front (3)	$\frac{3}{4}'' \times 6'' \times 33\frac{3}{8}''$
U	Drawer sides (6)	$\frac{3}{4}'' \times 6'' \times 20\frac{3}{4}''$
V	Drawer back (3)	$\frac{3}{4}'' \times 6'' \times 31\frac{3}{4}''$
W	Drawer bottom* (3)	$\frac{1}{4}'' \times 19\frac{1}{4}'' \times 31\frac{3}{4}''$

* Make these parts from plywood.

HARDWARE

#8 x 1½" Flathead wood screws (8)

#8 x 1¼" Flathead wood screws (6)

Knobs (8)

Drawer slides (3 pair)

Flipper door slides (2 sets)

Hinge set (2)

#16 x 1" Wire nails (24–30)

How do I build it?

PREPARING THE MATERIALS

For the most part, the entertainment center is made from cherry and cherry plywood. You can purchase cherry-veneer plywood on special order through most lumberyards and hardwood dealers. To build the center as Mary Jane designed it, you'll need one sheet of ¾-inch cherry plywood to make the sides and the upper fixed shelf, and one sheet of ¾-inch birch plywood for the vertical partitions and the lower fixed shelf. You'll also need a half-sheet (48 inches square) of ¼-inch cherry plywood for the door panels. The back and the drawer bottoms are ¼-inch birch plywood. We used ordinary birch plywood for the parts that aren't visible. This saved us some money.

Bust down the sheets, but cut the parts that you will be edging — sides, partitions, and fixed shelves — slightly wider than needed.

EDGING PLYWOOD There are two ways to cover the plies on the edge of a sheet of plywood.

■ Glue veneer tape to the edge. This is adequate for edges that won't see much wear and tear, but the veneer will easily be chipped if the piece is subjected to any hard use.

■ Cover the edges with strips of hardwood or veneer "banding." The material should be wide enough to overlap the surfaces of the plywood slightly. That way, when you sand or scrape to clean

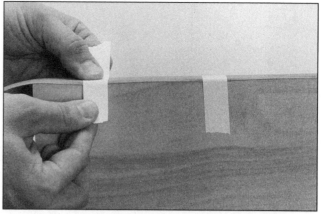

To cover the edge of a piece of plywood with veneer, cut the strips slightly wider than the plywood is thick. Inspect each strip to see which way it cups. Mark the concave side — this is the side you want to glue to the plywood. Apply glue to the plywood edge, then secure the veneer with masking tape. Masking tape is slightly elastic. If you use a strip every 3 to 4 inches, stretching the strip taut, it will generate enough clamping pressure to get a good bond. After the glue dries, trim the veneer flush with the faces of the plywood either by sanding it or by scraping it with a cabinet scraper.

up the glue joint and make the surfaces flush, you can remove a little stock from the edge material. If you have to remove any stock from the plywood, you risk cutting through the thin face veneer.

We elected to edge the plywood with hardwood strips. It wasn't that Jim and I expected the front edges of the case parts to see a lot of heavy action, but strips help simplify the joinery, as you'll see on page 92.

To cover a plywood edge with a hardwood strip, cut the strip to the width you want. The strips on the entertainment center are ¾ inch wide. Apply glue to the plywood edge and clamp the strip to it. As you tighten the clamps, feel with your fingers to make sure the strip is centered on the edge. Both faces should be just a little proud of the plywood. After the glue dries, scrape the strips flush with the plywood surface.

After covering and trimming the edge — whether you cover it with veneer or wood strips — trim the panels to their final dimensions. I find this is much easier than trying to apply the edging to the panels *after* they've been cut to size.

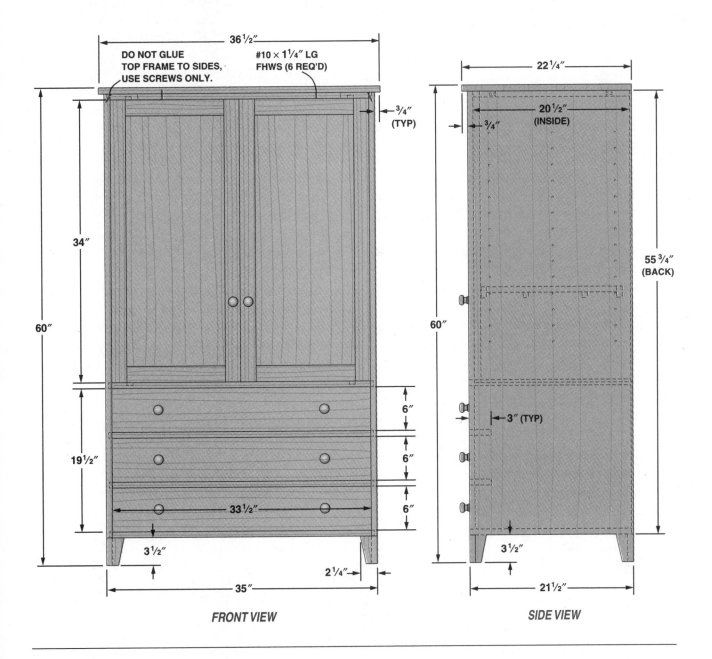

DO NOT GLUE TOP FRAME TO SIDES, USE SCREWS ONLY.

36½"

#10 × 1¼" LG FHWS (6 REQ'D)

¾" (TYP)

34"

60"

6"

6"

6"

19½"

33½"

3½"

2¼"

35"

FRONT VIEW

22¼"

20½" (INSIDE)

¾"

55¾" (BACK)

60"

3" (TYP)

3½"

21½"

SIDE VIEW

QUICK FIXTURES ■ *Sawing Grid and Circular Saw Guide*

The Sawing Grid fits over your sawhorses and provides better support for sheet materials than sawhorses alone. The grid prevents the sheet from bowing in the middle, no matter how you cut it up.

Make the grid from 2 × 4s, but don't fasten the parts together. Assemble the grid on the sawhorses whenever you need it. When it's just taking up space in your shop, take it apart and stack the pieces out of the way.

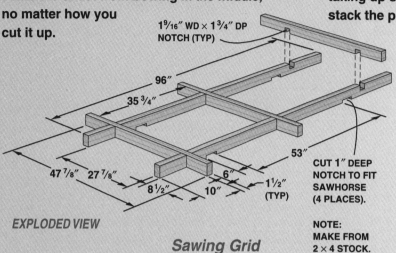

1⁹/₁₆" WD × 1³/₄" DP NOTCH (TYP)

96"

35³/₄"

53"

CUT 1" DEEP NOTCH TO FIT SAWHORSE (4 PLACES).

47⁷/₈" 27⁷/₈"

8¹/₂" 10"

6"

1¹/₂" (TYP)

EXPLODED VIEW

NOTE: MAKE FROM 2 × 4 STOCK.

Sawing Grid

TRY THIS!

Use the Sawing Grid when routing case joinery. The grid not only supports large parts, it makes it easier for you to attach guides, such as the T-Square Router Guide on page 13, to the work.

The Circular Saw Guide is an 8-foot-long straightedge that positions and guides a circular saw. Cut a base and a straightedge from plywood, using the *factory edges* (outside edges, cut at the factory) of the sheets to guide the cuts. Make the base about 3 inches wider than the base of your saw. Glue the parts together, using the factory edge on the ³/₄-inch strip as the guiding surface for the straightedge.

Note: Plywood edges are cut straight at the factory — usually. I've made several of these guides, and I've found it's always a good idea to sight down the edge of the plywood before I cut a strip I want to use as a straightedge. If there's a slight bow in the edge, I look for another sheet.

After the glue dries, trim the base to width using the circular saw blade you will use to cut the sheet materials. Once you have trimmed the base, you can use the sawed edge to

position the saw guide accurately. Place the guide on the "save" side of the layout line (opposite the waste), and

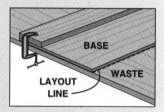

BASE

WASTE

LAYOUT LINE

position the edge of the base even with the line. Clamp the guide to the plywood and rest the circular saw on the base. Adjust the depth of cut so the blade will cut completely through the material and a fraction of an inch into the supporting grid. Make the cut, keeping the base of the saw firmly against the straightedge.

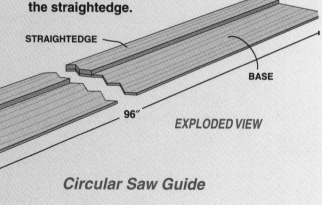

STRAIGHTEDGE

BASE

96"

EXPLODED VIEW

¹/₄" ³/₄" 3"

BASE OF YOUR SAW + 3"

Circular Saw Guide

METHODS OF WORK ■ *Cutting Plywood Sheets*

Cutting sheet materials is something of a nightmare for many craftsmen with small shops. For years, I thought I'd give my eyeteeth for a panel saw — and a place to put it. However, necessity is a mother, and through trial and error Jim and I developed a simple system for cutting sheet materials accurately with a circular saw.

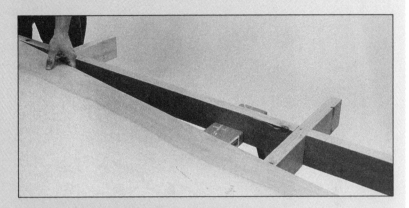

1 The most important part of the system is *support*. In order to cut a sheet accurately, you must properly support it. We lay each sheet on a *sawing grid* that supports the plywood on *both sides* of the cut. Adjust the depth of cut so the circular saw cuts completely through the material and bites just a little bit into the grid.

2 Rather than try to follow a layout line by eye, we guide the saw along a circular saw guide — a long, shop-made straightedge, as shown on the facing page. This keeps the saw perfectly straight on cuts up to 8 feet long. If you outfit your saw with a high-quality combination blade or plywood blade, you can make finish cuts with this jig.

3 Or, if you prefer, you can "double-cut." Slice the sheets into easily manageable pieces with the circular saw, then cut them to their final dimensions on a table saw. To do this, you must lay out the initial cuts so the parts will be a little larger than needed. Also be sure that each part has at least one straight factory edge. When you trim the sheets to their final dimensions, use the factory edge as the guiding edge for the first cut. **Tip: Make the first table saw cut slightly wide, then turn the sheet and trim the factory edge. Although factory edges are straight enough to use as a guiding edge, they are often too bunged up to use for joinery.**

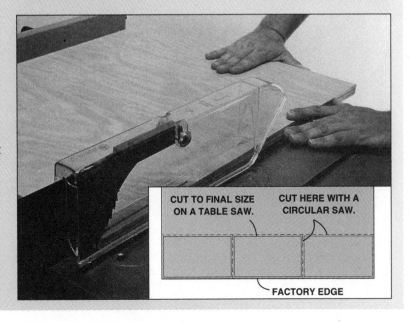

CUT TO FINAL SIZE ON A TABLE SAW.   CUT HERE WITH A CIRCULAR SAW.

FACTORY EDGE

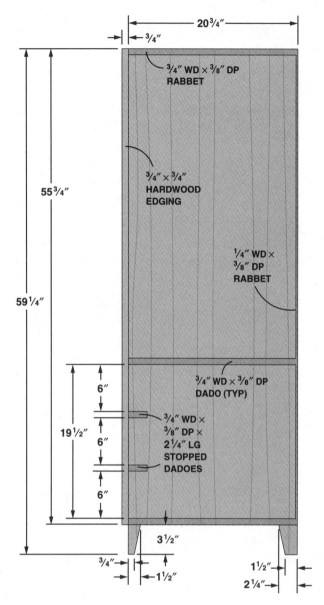

20¾"

¾"

¾" WD × ⅜" DP
RABBET

55¾"

¾" × ¾"
HARDWOOD
EDGING

59¼"

¼" WD ×
⅜" DP
RABBET

¾" WD × ⅜" DP
DADO (TYP)

6"

¾" WD ×
⅜" DP ×
2¼" LG
STOPPED
DADOES

19½"

6"

6"

3½"

¾"

1½"

1½"

2¼"

LEFT SIDE LAYOUT

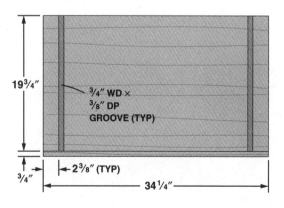

19¾"

¾" WD ×
⅜" DP
GROOVE (TYP)

¾"

2⅜" (TYP)

34¼"

MIDDLE SHELF LAYOUT

MAKING THE CASE JOINERY The case for the entertainment center contains nothing we haven't seen before, but some of the parts play a different role. There are two dividers or *partitions* in the case, and they support the adjustable shelves that hold the electronic components. But their purpose is not to reduce the span of the shelves. Instead, these partitions create cavities or *pockets* on either side of the case. As the doors open, they slide back into these pockets. Without the partitions, you couldn't mount shelves in the case; the pocket doors would interfere.

The case also has a web frame, but it's not used to support drawers. Instead, it secures the top to the case and is called a *top frame*. We drove screws up through the frame and into the top. This way, the screws weren't visible from the outside, and there were no screw holes to fill.

There are no structures or joinery inside the case that support the shelves. The drawer dividers are decorative; they serve only to set the drawers apart from one another visually as if they were resting on a frame. But instead, the drawers are hung on *full extension slides*, which mount directly to the sides of the case.

Making the Top Frame. Cut the grooves in the inside edges of the top frame's stiles (the parts that run side to side), and cut matching tongues in the ends of the rails (the parts that run front to back). Assemble the frame with glue, making sure it's square and flat.

Rout the stopped dadoes for the drawer dividers, starting at the front edge and stopping when the dadoes are only 2¼ inches long. Square the stopped ends with a chisel. After you apply the edging to the front edge, these dadoes will be stopped at *both* ends.

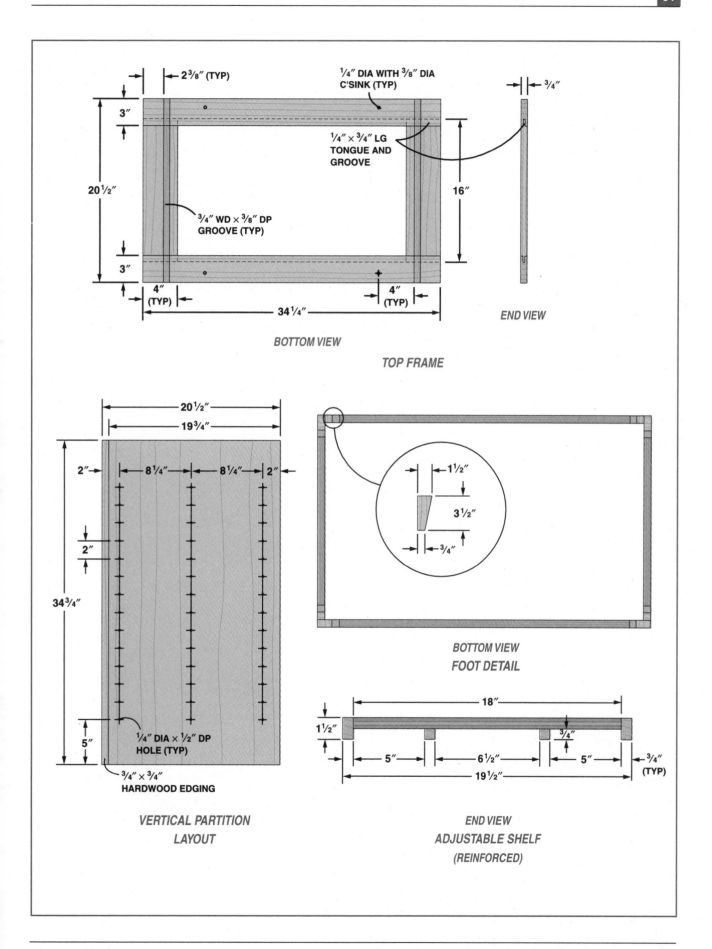

2³⁄₈″ (TYP)

¹⁄₄″ DIA WITH ³⁄₈″ DIA C'SINK (TYP)

³⁄₄″

3″

¹⁄₄″ × ³⁄₄″ LG TONGUE AND GROOVE

20¹⁄₂″

16″

³⁄₄″ WD × ³⁄₈″ DP GROOVE (TYP)

3″

4″ (TYP)

4″ (TYP)

34¹⁄₄″

BOTTOM VIEW

END VIEW

TOP FRAME

20¹⁄₂″

19³⁄₄″

2″

8¹⁄₄″

8¹⁄₄″

2″

1¹⁄₂″

3¹⁄₂″

2″

³⁄₄″

34³⁄₄″

5″

¹⁄₄″ DIA × ¹⁄₂″ DP HOLE (TYP)

³⁄₄″ × ³⁄₄″ HARDWOOD EDGING

BOTTOM VIEW

FOOT DETAIL

VERTICAL PARTITION LAYOUT

18″

1¹⁄₂″

³⁄₄″

5″

6¹⁄₂″

5″

³⁄₄″ (TYP)

19¹⁄₂″

END VIEW

ADJUSTABLE SHELF

(REINFORCED)

Making the Rabbets, Dadoes, and Notches. Cut or rout the horizontal joints in the plywood sides, middle shelf, and top frame. Then attach the edging strips to the sides and fixed shelves. This turns the dadoes, grooves, and rabbets into stopped joints — you can't see them at the front of the assembled cabinet. Trim the sides and shelves to the proper width, removing the stock from the back edges. Then rout the vertical rabbets in the sides that will hold the back.

Cut notches in the front corners of the drawer dividers to fit the stopped joints in the sides. Cut the edging on the fixed shelves ⅜ inch short of the front corners to create notches in these parts. These, too, fit the stopped joints.

MAKING THE ADJUSTABLE SHELF This is also a good time to make the adjustable shelf, since it also has to be edged with hardwood strips. If you plan to rest no more than one or two components on a shelf, you can simply cut a piece of plywood and cover the front edge with a ¾-inch × ¾-inch hardwood strip.

Shelves for heavy components, such as a television set or a heavy stack of audio components, must be reinforced so they won't sag. Edge them with a 1½-inch-wide strip at both the front and the back and attach ¾-inch × ¾-inch strips to the undersides, as shown in the *Adjustable Shelf–End View* on page 91.

After you've edged and trimmed the shelf, it should be just 19½ inches from front to back. This will leave a gap near the back for ventilation — we'll talk about that in just a bit.

Drilling the Shelving Support Holes. The adjustable shelf in this project is supported on pins, and the pins rest in stopped holes in the partitions. Drill the holes with the aid of a hole-spacing guide.

Look Here! For instructions on how to make a hole-spacing guide, see page 17.

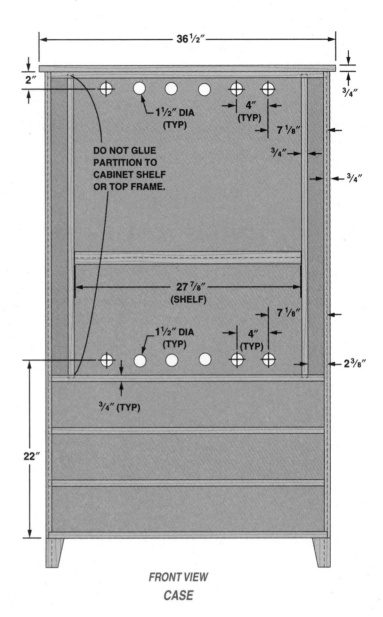

FRONT VIEW
CASE

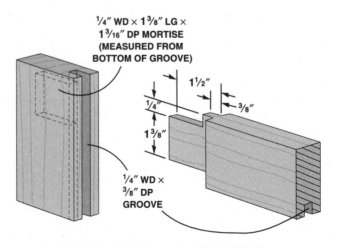

HAUNCHED MORTISE-AND-TENON DETAIL

CUTTING THE FEET The "feet" on this piece are just cutout shapes. Lay out the cutouts for the feet in the sides, as shown in the *Side View* on page 87, and cut them with a saber saw or coping saw. Cut the front feet from hardwood.

ASSEMBLING THE CASE

Dry assemble the case and set out the clamps you'll need. Then attach the sides, fixed shelves, top frame, and dividers with glue. Also glue the front feet to the sides and bottom shelf.

Slide the partitions into their grooves in the middle shelf and the top frame. Tack the back on with a few brads, and rest the top on the top frame. However, *don't* attach the partitions, back, or top permanently at this time. Wait until after you have installed the doors and drawers *and* applied a finish. The reason for this is that you're going to find it almost impossible to install the door and drawer hardware without removing the back and the partitions. Furthermore, you'll need to install the hardware *twice* — once when you fit the doors and drawers and again after you finish the cabinet.

MAKING AND HANGING THE DOORS The doors on the entertainment center are inset frame-and-panel doors. Like the door on the spice cupboard, we elected to join the door frames with haunched mortise-and-tenon joints. The grooves around the inside edges of the rails and stiles hold the flat door panels. Note that the inside edges of the outside door stiles are chamfered. This is required by the hardware on which the doors will be mounted.

Assemble the frame members with glue, but let the panels float in the grooves. You don't have to allow as much room for the door panels to expand and contract, since they are made from plywood. Plywood is much more stable than solid wood. But it does move a small amount, and for this reason, it's not a good idea to glue the panels in place.

Hanging Pocket Doors. Unlike ordinary doors, which are hung on the sides of the case or the face frame, the doors on this cabinet are each hinged to a pocket door slide. This slide is attached to a cabinet side. When you open the doors, they travel backwards along the slides, disappearing into the pockets.

It sounds like a complex system, but it's not. It's actually a combination of two simple systems — slides and hinges. And the installation is reasonably simple, too. Install the slides inside the cabinet, attach the hinges to the doors, then hang the doors on the slides.

> **Look Here!** For more information on making frame-and-panel doors, see page 20; making a haunched mortise-and-tenon joint, see page 21; assembling a door, see page 25.

DOOR LAYOUT

16³⁄₄″
15³⁄₄″
2″
¹⁄₄″ WD × ³⁄₈″ DP GROOVE (TYP)
30³⁄₄″ (PANEL)
34″
10″
2″
13¹⁄₂″ (PANEL)

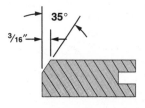

35°
³⁄₁₆″

OUTSIDE DOOR STILE
CHAMFER DETAIL

METHODS OF WORK ■ *Hanging Pocket Doors*

Pocket doors (also called *flipper doors*) are hinged to slides, and the slides are mounted to the cabinet sides. This arrangement lets you push the open doors back into the cabinet. To hang a pocket door, mount the slides, install the hinges, then attach the hinges to the slides.

1 Each *pocket door slide* is actually a set of slides — a top slide and a bottom slide. Mount the top slide at the top of the cabinet side and the bottom one at the bottom. Both slides must be parallel to one another.

2 Cut a wooden tie bar to the proper length and mount it to the top and bottom slides. This ties the slides together so they move as one. Test the sliding action by pushing and pulling on the tie bar. If the action isn't smooth and one of the slides binds, they aren't parallel. Loosen the screws and adjust them so the action is smooth.

3 Measure the distance between the brackets, then mark the position of the hinge cups on the inside face of each door stile. Drill a 1⅜-inch-diameter, ½-inch-deep (135 millimeters × 13 millimeters) hole at each location. (There are special drill bits available for this operation, or you can use a 1⅜-inch Forstner bit.)

4 Attach the hinge cups to the door, then slide the arm on the hinge cups into the brackets and tighten the locking screws. Adjust the hinges so the doors are properly aligned when closed. Finally, install the guides in the case, near the bottom edges of the door. Position the guides even with (or just a little to the inside of) the partitions. Set them back from the edge of the case precisely the width of the doors. This hardware guides the doors when you push them back into the case, and it positions the doors when you pull them out again and close them.

MAKING AND HANGING THE DRAWERS The drawers in this entertainment center are all the same depth — 5½ inches inside with 6-inch-wide fronts. This is not the most visually pleasing arrangement. As I mentioned on page 32, repetitive elements in a design — in this case, the three drawers — look better if the sizes follow a definite progression with the largest drawer at the bottom. And Mary Jane would have designed it this way but for other practical considerations.

We wanted all three drawers to hold videocassettes, stored on edge so we could read the spines. If the bottom drawer were deeper, there would be wasted space in the cabinet. And if the top drawer were shallower, it would reduce the number of cassettes the entertainment center would store. Mary Jane decided to let function dictate form here, even though it violated a few design rules. Oftentimes, you have to make tradeoffs like these when designing a cabinet.

Making the Drawer Joinery. The front corners of the drawers are assembled with lock joints; the remaining parts are joined with either grooves or dadoes. In this particular design, the front tongue in the lock joint protrudes ½ inch on either side of the drawer, as shown in the *Drawer–Top View*. This creates a "face" that hides the hardware on which the drawers hang. Almost all extension slides require ½ inch of space on each side of the drawer.

Hanging the Drawers. As I mentioned, the drawers hang on full extension slides. Most extension slides allow you to pull the drawers about two-thirds of the way out of the case. Full extension slides let you pull them out all the way. They are slightly more expensive than regular slides, but they are worth the money when you need to reach small or slender items at the back of a drawer.

Both regular extension slides and full extension slides are installed in the same manner. The slides come apart in two pieces — the slide itself, which attaches to the inside surface of the case, and a mount, which attaches to the side of the drawer. The whole trick in installing this hardware is to measure and mark a line on the side of the case were you will attach the hardware and a corresponding line on the drawer side. Both should be aligned vertically. But don't worry if you install one piece of hardware or the other a little off the mark. Both are mounted on elongated slots, allowing you to adjust their position up and down a fraction of an inch.

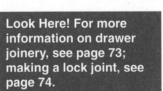

Look Here! For more information on drawer joinery, see page 73; making a lock joint, see page 74.

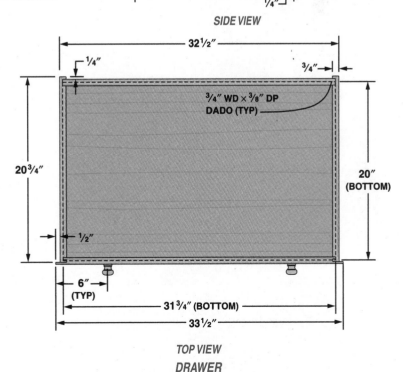

SIDE VIEW

TOP VIEW
DRAWER

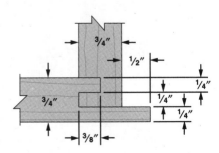

LOCK JOINT DETAIL

METHODS OF WORK ■ *Installing Extension Slides*

To hang a drawer on extension slides, screw the slides to the sides of the drawer and to the inside surface of the case. To do this, you must first take apart the slides. Remove the mounting brackets from the slides.

RESOURCES

You can purchase both regular and full extension slides from most mail-order woodworking suppliers, including:

The Woodworkers' Store
4365 Willow Drive
Medina, MN 55340

1   **Measure and mark** the position of the slides on the inside surface of the case and the mounting brackets on the sides of the drawer. Although you can position the hardware anywhere, most craftsmen prefer to mount the slides near the bottom edges of the drawer. Let's say you have a drawer that fits its opening with a ¹⁄₁₆-inch gap top and bottom. Measure up 1 inch from the bottom edge of the drawer side and make a mark — that's where you want to place the mounting bracket. Then measure up 1¹⁄₁₆ inches from the bottom of the drawer opening on the case — that's where you want the slides.

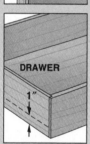

2 **Draw horizontal lines** at the mark and drill pilot holes along the lines for the screws that hold the hardware in place.

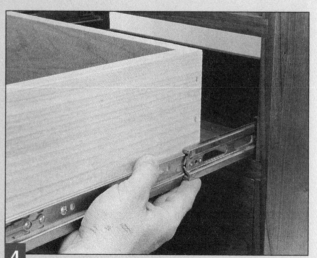

3 **Attach the mounting brackets** to both sides of the drawer and attach the slides to the inside of the case on each side of the drawer opening.

4 **Snap the mounting brackets** to the slides and test the action of the drawers. If the drawer binds as you pull it in and out, the slides aren't parallel. Detach the brackets from the slides, loosen the mounting screws, and adjust the position of the hardware.

SHOP SAVVY ■ *Ventilating a Cabinet*

When building cabinets for audio, video, gaming, and computer equipment, you face a special challenge. These electronic components generate heat that can build up in the enclosed spaces and harm the equipment or shorten its useful life. To prevent this, you must *ventilate* the enclosures to exhaust the heat.

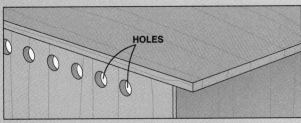

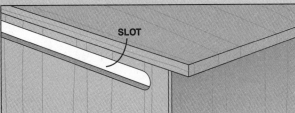

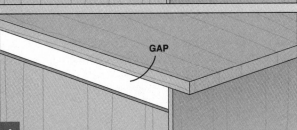

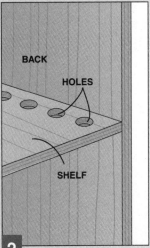 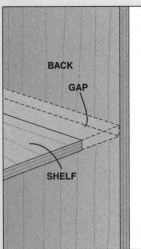

1 When designing a ventilation system for your cabinet, remember that hot air rises. The best place to exhaust it is at the top of the case. There are three easy ways to do this. Drill a row of 1- to 2-inch-diameter holes in the back, near the top edge *(top)*. Rout a 1-inch slot in the back, near the top edge *(middle)*. Make the back slightly shorter than you would otherwise, and mount it to leave a 1-inch gap at the top *(bottom)*. Warning: If you plan to operate the electronics with the doors closed, make an equal number of ventilation holes, slots, or gaps in the *bottom* of the case to draw cool air into it.

2 Not only must you exhaust hot air from the top of the cabinet and draw cool air in from the bottom, you must also prevent the hot air from becoming trapped between the shelves. To do this, drill a row of 1-inch-diameter holes near the back edge of each shelf *(left)* or cut each shelf 1 inch narrower than the depth of the case and mount it so there's a 1-inch-wide gap at the back *(right)*.

3 If you're operating a lot of electronics in the cabinet or they are particularly sensitive to heat, you may not wish to rely on passive ventilation. Instead, mount one or two *muffin fans* in the back of the cabinet, near the top. These fans are very quiet, and they can be wired to operate when you turn on the electronics. They are available at most electronics supply stores.

SHOP SAVVY ■ *Wiring a Cabinet*

To operate electronic equipment in a cabinet, you'll need to provide it with electrical power. Additionally, it's a good idea to organize the power cords, patch cords, cables, and other wire to avoid a dangerous and confusing tangle.

1   **Perhaps the easiest way** to provide power for electrical components is to mount a *plug strip* inside the case and run all the power cords to it. The strip should have a built-in circuit breaker to prevent an electrical overload. In addition, it should provide "surge protection" against lightning strikes or sudden spikes in the current. These surges can wipe out delicate circuitry. Locate the strip where you can reach it easily, and orient the switch so you can use it to turn all the components off and on at once.

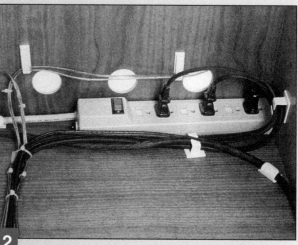

2   **To organize power cables,** purchase plastic "cable keepers" and install them inside the cabinet where you want to run the wires. There are many different types of keepers available; these are just a few I picked up at a local electronics supply store.

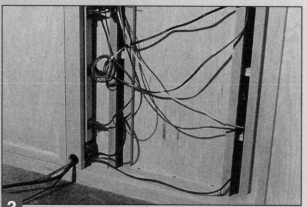

3   **Another way to organize wires and cords** is to build a "wiring run." Runs can be channels that go down the sides or the back of the cabinet, but one of the easiest ways to make a run is to build your cabinet with a false back. Run the wires through the space between the false back and the real one. Build a door in the real back or make it removable so you can access the wires easily.

4   **Should you want to add lighting** to your cabinet, there are special lights made just for this purpose. Mount them at the top of the cabinet. If you wish to hide them from view, put them behind a baffle. Remember, lights generate heat, too. Ventilate the top of the cabinet above the lights.

FINISHING THE ENTERTAINMENT CENTER

Once the doors and drawers are installed on their hardware, I know you won't be able to resist putting the cabinet all together, even though there's no reason to do so just yet. The cabinet needs to be finished before you can put it together permanently. However, I can never resist the temptation to see how it's going to look when it's completely done, and Jim can't either. So go ahead and slide the partitions back into their grooves. Attach the top with wood screws, and tack the back to the case with brads. Don't drive the brads all the way home, however. Finally, install the adjustable shelf.

After you've called in everyone in a 10-mile radius to admire your craftsmanship, it's time to get back to work. Remove the top, back, shelves, and partitions. Also remove the doors, drawers, and hardware. Set all the metal parts aside and apply a finish to the wooden ones. Jim and I used a water-based varnish for this project. It goes on quickly, and it's easy to sand between coats.

However, the same caution applies that I mentioned when I was describing the finish we put on the mission bookcase: When applying a water-based finish, you can save yourself a lot of grief by raising the grain beforehand. After a final sanding, wipe the wood down with a wet rag and let it dry. Then sand again with the last grit you used.

Once you have finished your cabinet, put it back together. This time you can attach the back with brads and partitions with wood screws. However, I'd suggest that you still refrain from gluing them in place. You may want to remove them someday to repair the slides.

> **Look Here!** For more information on raising wood grain, see page 46.

METHODS OF WORK ■ *Applying a Nitric Acid Stain*

Although I chose not to stain this project, I know that many craftsmen prefer to stain cherry. The new wood is very light, and it takes several months for a dark patina to develop. Rather than wait, many of us go ahead and apply a stain.

The trouble is, staining cherry can be a nightmare. The wood takes stains and dyes unevenly, and the result is often blotchy. There are several solutions to this dilemma, but one of the easiest is to stain the wood with *nitric acid.* The acid speeds up the natural aging process, oxidizing the surface and creating a rich, dark patina. What's more, the color is absolutely even.

You can buy nitric acid at most chemical supply houses and businesses that sell pool-maintenance supplies. Ask for *laboratory-grade* nitric acid. (If you get the industrial grade, you'll have to buy it in 30-gallon drums.) Dilute the acid 7 parts distilled water to 1 part acid.

Apply the acid to a small area of the wood surface (1–2 square feet) with an old brush, and let it soak in for a few minutes. Warm the area you've stained with a heat gun. Keep the gun moving to heat the wood evenly and keep from scorching the surface. In a few moments, the color will suddenly "develop." Repeat until you have stained the entire surface. Note: The color will *not* appear without the application of heat.

SAFEGUARD

To prevent a dangerous thermal reaction, always pour the acid into the water, not the other way around. Wear a full face shield and rubber gloves when mixing and using this chemical stain.

Built-In Bathroom Vanity

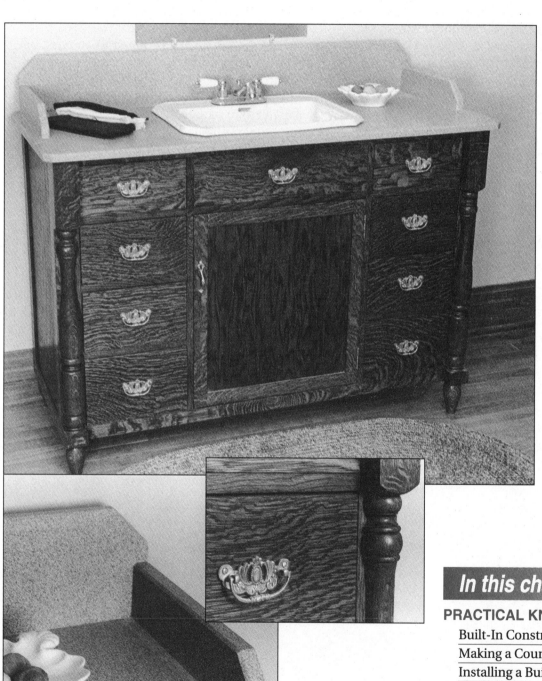

The bathroom vanity is a built-in with a twist. The mission bookcase (page 30) was more typical. The case was standard construction for a built-in. This vanity, however, shows other possibilities. It's a built-in, sure enough — because of the plumbing, it has to be anchored to the wall. But it's designed to look like a Victorian washstand. The plywood case is made the same as most built-ins, but appliqués on the sides make it look like old-time frame-and-panel construction. The *toe space* — the recessed area at the base that prevents you from stubbing your toe as you stand at the cabinet — is much deeper than it would be otherwise, giving the illusion that the cabinet is supported solely by its feet. These illusions are a new trend in cabinetmaking. Designers of high-class interiors have begun to disguise built-ins to look like fine furniture. This project will show you some of their tricks.

What size should it be?

Like other cabinets, built-ins are sized to hold specific items. In this case, Mary Jane designed the vanity to hold toiletries. But just as important, built-ins are also designed to fit the space in which they are installed. This cabinet had to fit in a 54-inch-wide area between a wall and a shower enclosure in a Victorian bathroom. So Mary Jane designed it to be 50 inches wide, leaving 2 inches on either side.

> **Look Here!** For more information on standard sizes for built-in cabinets, see page 49.

What style will it be?

There are two common ways to design and build built-in units. However, you aren't limited to just these two options. With a little imagination — and the use of a few appliqués, you can create almost any style.

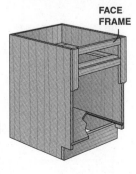

TRADITIONAL STYLE

Traditional built-in cabinets have face frames. The doors that enclose them are hinged to the frames, like the mission bookcase on page 30. The doors and drawers are usually either inset or lipped.

FACE FRAME

CONTEMPORARY STYLE

Contemporary built-ins have no face frames. The doors are hinged directly to the case sides, and usually overlay the cases.

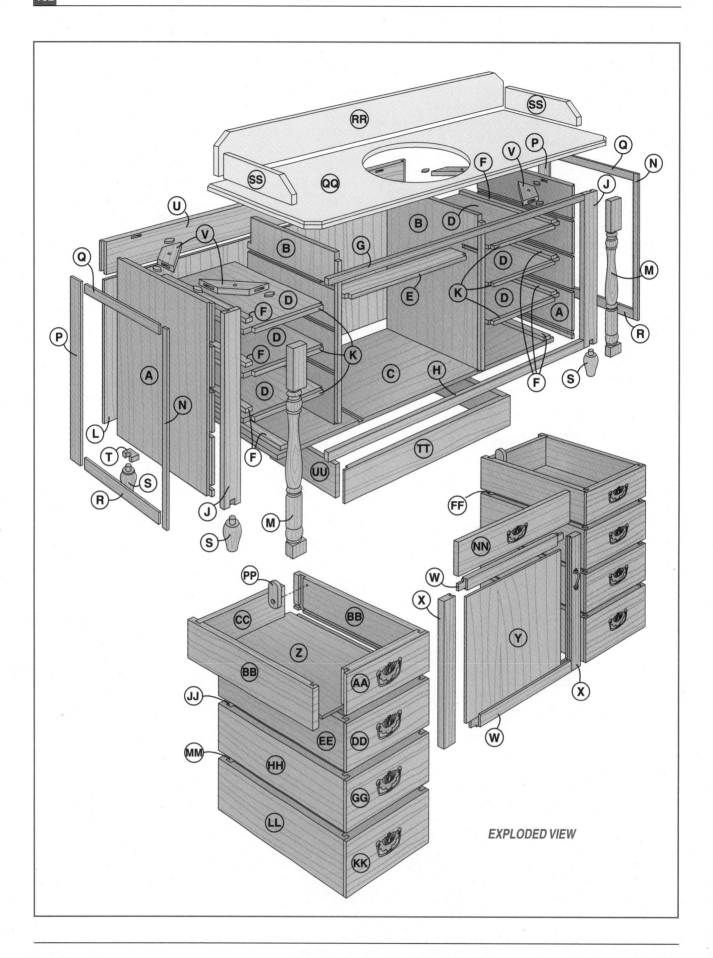

EXPLODED VIEW

BUILT-IN BATHROOM VANITY ■ MATERIALS LIST

PARTS

A	Sides* (2)	¾″ × 17⅞″ × 29¼″
B	Dividers* (2)	¾″ × 17¼″ × 28⅛″
C	Bottom*	¾″ × 17¼″ × 46¾″
D	Horizontal partitions* (6)	¾″ × 13¼″ × 17¼″
E	Center rail	¾″ × 3″ × 20¼″
F	Drawer guides (8)	¾″ × 1½″ × 17¼″
G	Face frame top	¾″ × 1″ × 43″
H	Face frame bottom	¾″ × 1½″ × 43″
J	Face frame stiles (2)	¾″ × 2¼″ × 29¼″
K	Face frame edging (6)	¾″ × ¾″ × 11″
L	Back*	¼″ × 25⅝″ × 46¾″
M	Split turnings (2)	1¼″ × 2½″ × 29¼″
N	Vertical front side trim (2)	¼″ × 1¼″ × 29¼″
P	Vertical rear side trim (2)	¼″ × 2½″ × 29¼″
Q	Horizontal top side trim (2)	¼″ × 1″ × 14½″
R	Horizontal bottom side trim (2)	¼″ × 1½″ × 14½″
S	Feet (4)	2½″ dia. × 5″
T	Rear foot spacer	¾″ × 1½″ × 2¼″
U	Nailing strip	¾″ × 4″ × 46¾″
V	Corner cleats (4)	¾″ × 3″ × 9¼″
W	Door rails (2)	¾″ × 1½″ × 18¾″
X	Door stiles (2)	¾″ × 1½″ × 20⅞″
Y	Door panel*	¼″ × 17⅛″ × 18⅝″
Z	Drawer bottoms* (8)	¼″ × 10⅜″ × 16¾″
AA	Top drawer fronts (2)	¾″ × 4¹⁵⁄₁₆″ × 10⅞″
BB	Top drawer sides (4)	½″ × 4¹⁵⁄₁₆″ × 17¾″
CC	Top drawer backs (2)	½″ × 4¹⁵⁄₁₆″ × 10⅜″
DD	Upper middle drawer fronts (2)	¾″ × 5¹⁵⁄₁₆″ × 10⅞″
EE	Upper middle drawer sides (4)	½″ × 5¹⁵⁄₁₆″ × 17¾″
FF	Upper middle drawer backs (2)	½″ × 5¹⁵⁄₁₆″ × 10⅜″
GG	Lower middle drawer fronts (2)	¾″ × 6³⁄₁₆″ × 10⅞″
HH	Lower middle drawer sides (4)	½″ × 6³⁄₁₆″ × 17¾″
JJ	Lower middle drawer backs (2)	½″ × 6³⁄₁₆″ × 10⅜″
KK	Bottom drawer fronts (2)	¾″ × 7³⁄₁₆″ × 10⅞″
LL	Bottom drawer sides (4)	½″ × 7³⁄₁₆″ × 17¾″
MM	Bottom drawer backs (2)	½″ × 7³⁄₁₆″ × 10⅜″
NN	False drawer front	¾″ × 5″ × 19½″
PP	Drawer kickers (2)	¾″ × 1″ × 2″
QQ	Countertop‡	¾″ × 20½″ × 50″
RR	Backsplash‡	¾″ × 6″ × 48″
SS	Sidesplashes‡ (2)	¾″ × 3″ × 13″
TT	Base front	¾″ × 4¾″ × variable
UU	Base sides (2)	¾″ × 4¾″ × variable

* Make these parts from plywood.

‡ Make these parts from particleboard.

HARDWARE

#20 Biscuits (8)

#6 × ¾″ Flathead wood screws (2)

#16 × 1″ Wire nails (24–30)

#10 × 1½″ Flathead wood screws (4)

Drawer pulls (9)

Door pull

1⅜″ × 2½″ Hinge (1 pair)

Magnetic catch

½″ wd. × 10 ft. Teflon tape (6 rolls)

Plastic laminate (15 sq. ft.)

How do I build it?

PREPARING THE MATERIALS

Most built-in cabinets are made from plywood, and this one is no exception. All the major case parts are made from plywood — there are three sheets of ¾-inch plywood in this vanity, as well as a sheet of ¼-inch plywood for the door panel, drawer bottoms, and back.

The plywood parts that show on the outside are white oak-veneered plywood, which Jim special-ordered from a hardwood supplier. The solid wood parts are also made

> **Look Here!** For more information on cutting plywood sheets, see page 89.

SHOP SAVVY

To estimate the number of plywood sheets it will take to build a project, first make up a cutting list, similar to the Materials List shown on page 103. Multiply the length and width (in inches) of each plywood part to get the *surface area* in square inches. Total the surface areas of those parts of the same thickness, then divide by 4608, the surface area of a standard 48-inch x 96-inch sheet. Round up the answer to the nearest whole sheet.

from white oak. Mary Jane designed the cabinet to have the appearance of a Victorian washstand, and white oak was a favorite wood of the period.

Plane the solid stock to ¾ inch thick, then bust down the lumber and the sheets. Be sure to "true" the stock for the door frame members, jointing and planing it as straight as possible.

MAKING THE CASE

The case is slightly different from what you've seen in other chapters, and not just because the cabinet is built-in. Ordinarily, the drawers would have been hung on slides, much like the drawers in the entertainment center, or set on web frames like the drawer in the Chippendale china cabinet. Good slides, however, are expensive. And with the white oak plywood and laminated top, the cost of this project was already getting out of hand. Additionally, web frames are time-consuming to make, and we would have needed a zillion of them (well, six, anyway) for this project. So, to save time and money, we decided to simply rest them on fixed plywood shelves.

BUILT-IN CONSTRUCTION Ordinarily, a built-in case is made much like a freestanding cabinet case, with a few exceptions, as I mentioned on page 48. The most important of these is a *nailing strip* to attach the case to the wall.

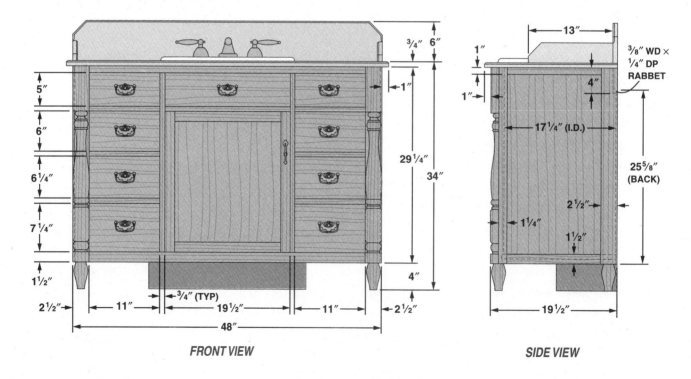

FRONT VIEW   *SIDE VIEW*

The base on most built-in cabinets is incorporated into the case. On this cabinet, however, it's a separate assembly. Additionally, the toe space is much deeper than is common. Mary Jane wanted to set the toe-board back as far as possible so the cabinet would appear as a freestanding washstand. But we still needed a small base to enclose the plumbing.

ANOTHER WAY TO GO

Mary Jane's design requires a few turned parts — the feet and the applied split turnings. This may present a problem to you, especially if you don't have a lathe. However, there are other alternatives.

You might use a different design for both the feet and the appliqués. Make the feet square or tapered, and use an ornate molding to decorate the face of the outside face frame stiles.

Or purchase turnings from a mail-order supplier that specializes in furniture parts, such as:

Adams Wood Products
974 Forest Drive
Morristown, TN 37814

Look Here! For more information on nailing strips, see page 48.

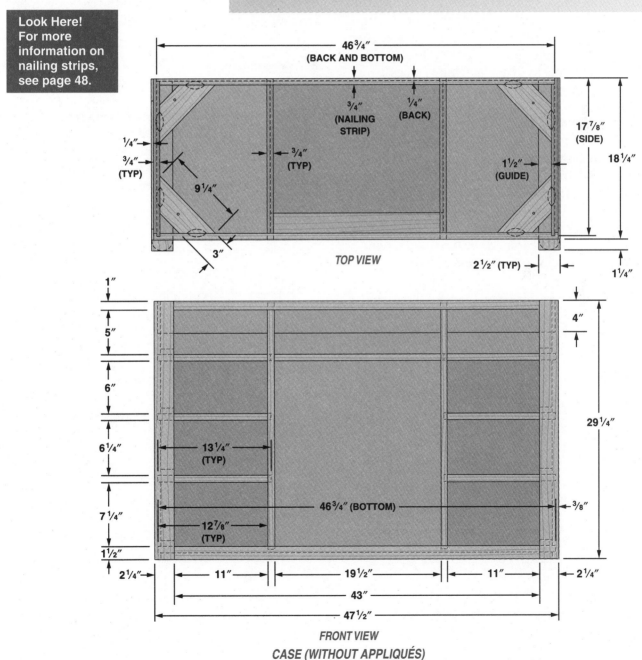

TOP VIEW

FRONT VIEW
CASE (WITHOUT APPLIQUÉS)

MAKING THE CASE JOINERY The case goes together much the same way as I described in the Entertainment Center chapter. The plywood pieces are edged and joined in a similar manner. However, there are some important differences.

First, cut the rabbets and dadoes that join the parts, as shown in the *Side Layout–Left Side* and *Divider Layout–Left Side*. (The right side and right divider are mirror images of the left parts.) Also cut a groove in the back face of the outside face frame stiles, as shown in the *Top View* on page 105. With one exception, none of these joints are stopped; most of the dadoes, rabbets, and grooves run from edge to edge or end to end. Note that the sides are also rabbeted at both the front *and* the back. These front rabbets create stub tenons that fit into the grooves in the backs of the face frame stiles.

After cutting the joinery, apply the ¾-inch × ¾-inch solid wood edging strips to the front edges of the dividers and fixed shelves (horizontal partitions). Note that the wood strips do not cover the full length of the front edges but stop short of the ends, as shown in the *Horizontal Partition Layout* and *Divider Layout–Left Side*. This creates notches at the front corners of the partitions and the top corners of the dividers.

These notches fit around the face frame members and the edging on adjoining parts. You'll also have to notch the back edges of the dividers to fit around the nailing strip.

The counter is held to the case by the cleats at the four corners, as shown in the *Top View* on page 105. Drive screws up through the cleats and into the underside of the counter when it's time to install it. (It's not time now.) The cleats themselves are attached to the sides, face frame, and nailing strip with biscuit joints. You have a choice — you can cut these joints before or after you assemble the case. Jim did it before he put the case together; I think I'd prefer afterward — different strokes.

> **Look Here! For more information on edging plywood, see page 86.**

ANOTHER WAY TO GO

If you don't have a biscuit joiner, attach the cleats with splines. Using a router and a slot cutter, rout ¼-inch-wide, ⅜-inch-deep slots in the sides, top face frame rail, and nailing strip where you will joint the cleat. Rout matching slots in the ends of the cleats. Make the splines from ¼-inch-thick, ¾-inch-wide strips of plywood.

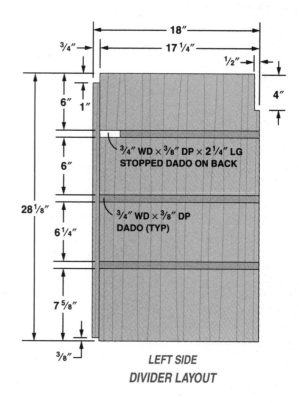

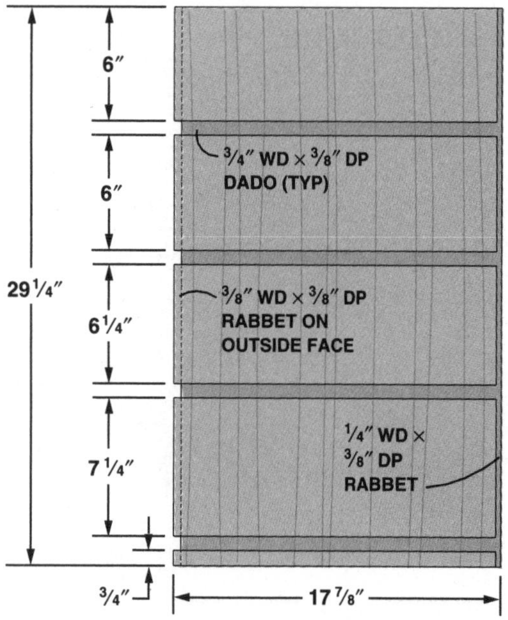

LEFT SIDE
SIDE LAYOUT

6"

6"

29¼"

6¼"

7¼"

¾" WD × ⅜" DP DADO (TYP)

⅜" WD × ⅜" DP RABBET ON OUTSIDE FACE

¼" WD × ⅜" DP RABBET

¾" 17⅞"

LEFT SIDE
DIVIDER LAYOUT

18"

¾" 17¼"

½"

6" 1"

4"

6"

28⅛"

6¼"

7⅝"

¾" WD × ⅜" DP × 2¼" LG STOPPED DADO ON BACK

¾" WD × ⅜" DP DADO (TYP)

⅜"

ASSEMBLING THE CASE

The assembly is a real bear, so you'll want to get someone to help you when putting it all together.

First, put the plywood parts together. Dry assemble the sides, dividers, partitions, center rail, and nailing strip to check the fit of the joinery and to set the clamps. Then assemble the case for real, gluing the parts together all at once. To keep the case square, attach the back with brads. *Don't* drive the brads all the way home just yet.

Once the glue sets on the case, lay the face frame parts in place to check the fit. Large cases have an annoying habit of growing or shrinking a fraction of an inch as you assemble them. On my first few case pieces, I made the mistake of gluing up the face frames first, only to find they didn't quite fit once the cases were assembled. I thought I was mismeasuring something, but a more experienced craftsman tipped me off that I was simply doing things in the wrong order.

Trim the face frame parts to fit the case. Assemble the outside face frame stiles, top rail, and bottom rail with dowels or pocket screws and glue. When the assembly is dry, glue it to the front of the case.

Remove the back and attach the nailing strip to the sides and dividers with glue and screws. Then reattach the back with brads. This time, drive the brads all the way home.

Assemble the base frame with glue and wood screws. Counterbore the screws and cover the heads with wooden plugs. Don't attach the base to the cabinet yet — wait until you have installed the project and run the plumbing.

Glue the drawer guides in place to the partitions, butting them up against the sides. These guide the drawers as you slide them in and out of the cabinet, keeping them traveling in a straight line.

Finally, attach the middle drawer front. Because there is a sink in this cabinet, this is a false drawer front — there's no drawer behind it. Jim attached it to the face frame and dividers permanently with glue and glue blocks. However, you could also attach it to a fall front tray to provide a little extra storage.

RESOURCES

Fall front tray hardware (also called sink front trays) are available from:
The Woodworkers' Store
4365 Willow Drive
Medina, MN 55340

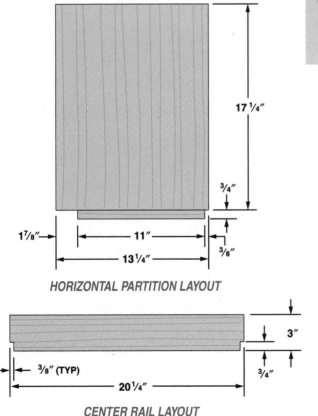

HORIZONTAL PARTITION LAYOUT

CENTER RAIL LAYOUT

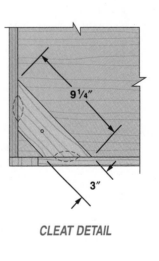

CLEAT DETAIL

MAKING AND INSTALLING THE DOOR AND DRAWERS

The case has inset drawers on each side and a frame-and-panel inset door in the center.

MAKING THE DOOR As he did when making the door on the spice cupboard and the entertainment center, Jim joined the frame members with haunched mortise-and-tenon joints. The grooves around the inside edges of the rails and stiles hold the flat door panel. Assemble the frame members with glue, but let the panel float in the grooves.

MAKING THE DRAWERS The front corners of the drawers are assembled with lock joints, as shown in the *Lock Joint Detail*. The back corners are fitted with dadoes; and the bottoms fit in a groove. Glue up the front, back, and sides for each drawer, but let the bottom "float." Don't glue it; let the bottom expand and contract in its grooves.

HANGING THE DOORS AND DRAWERS Jim hung the cabinet door on butt hinges, cutting hinge mortises in the door frame and the case. We decided to hold the door closed with a simple magnetic catch.

To hang the drawers, all you need to do is fit them to the openings. Check the sliding action to make sure they can be pulled in and out of the case easily. If they bind, remove a little stock from the sides with a hand plane or belt sander.

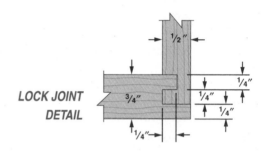

LOCK JOINT DETAIL

Look Here! For more information on making frame-and-panel doors, see page 20; making a haunched mortise-and-tenon joint, see page 21; assembling a door, see page 25; drawer joinery or making a lock joint, see page 74.

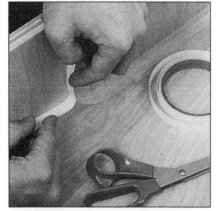

To let the drawers slide as smoothly as possible, apply Teflon tape to the bottom edges of the sides and the faces of the sides near the bottom. It's best to do this *after* you have fitted the drawers and applied a finish to the project. **Note: You can purchase Teflon tape through most woodworking suppliers.**

SHOP SAVVY

When fitting a drawer — or any assembly of solid wood — in an opening, take into account the time of year. In the summer, in most locations, the weather is as humid as it gets all year, and the wood has expanded as much as it's going to. You can fit the assemblies fairly close. In the winter, the weather is dry and the wood has shrunk. You must fit the drawers a little looser or they will stick when they swell in the summer. When in doubt, remove less stock rather than more. If the drawers begin to stick later in the year, you can always fit them again.

TRY THIS!

It's sometimes difficult to tell what surface to plane when a drawer is binding. After all, you can't see the surfaces that rub together. You can, however, get a pretty good idea by rubbing a pencil lead on the surface you suspect, coloring it fairly black. Then slide the drawer into the case. Pull it out again and look inside the case. If you guessed right, the darkened surface of the drawer will leave a mark inside the case where it rubs. Later, you can sand away the pencil marks.

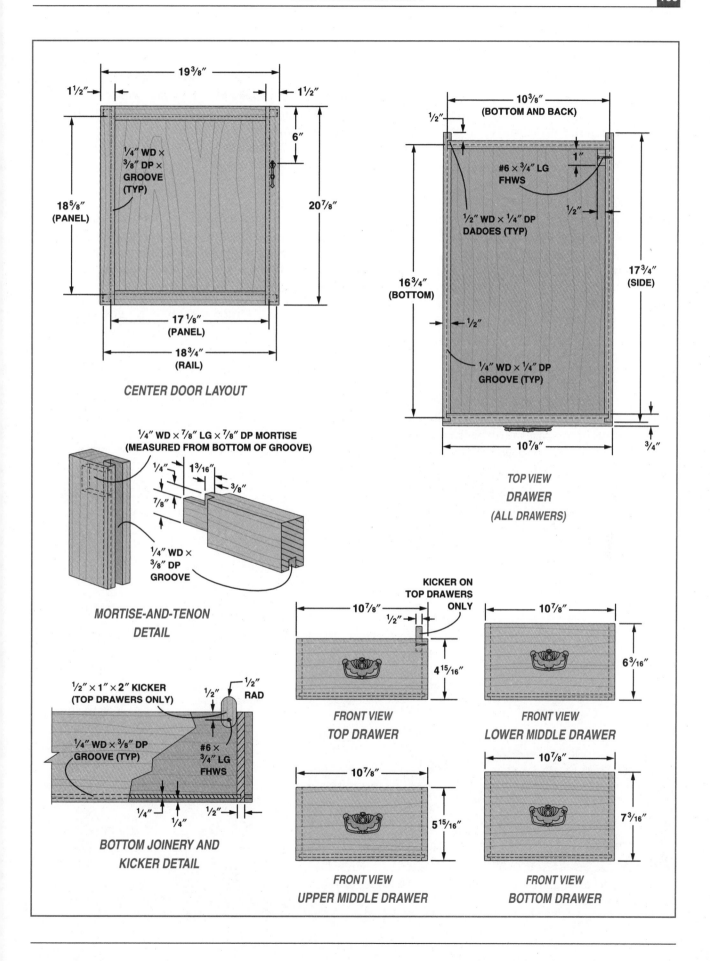

CENTER DOOR LAYOUT

19³/₈″
1¹/₂″
1¹/₂″
6″
¹/₄″ WD × ³/₈″ DP × GROOVE (TYP)
18⁵/₈″ (PANEL)
20⁷/₈″
17¹/₈″ (PANEL)
18³/₄″ (RAIL)

10³/₈″ (BOTTOM AND BACK)
¹/₂″
#6 × ³/₄″ LG FHWS
1″
¹/₂″ WD × ¹/₄″ DP DADOES (TYP)
¹/₂″
16³/₄″ (BOTTOM)
17³/₄″ (SIDE)
¹/₂″
¹/₄″ WD × ¹/₄″ DP GROOVE (TYP)
10⁷/₈″
³/₄″

TOP VIEW
DRAWER
(ALL DRAWERS)

¹/₄″ WD × ⁷/₈″ LG × ⁷/₈″ DP MORTISE (MEASURED FROM BOTTOM OF GROOVE)
¹/₄″
1³/₁₆″
³/₈″
⁷/₈″
¹/₄″ WD × ³/₈″ DP GROOVE

MORTISE-AND-TENON DETAIL

¹/₂″ × 1″ × 2″ KICKER (TOP DRAWERS ONLY)
¹/₂″
¹/₂″ RAD
¹/₄″ WD × ³/₈″ DP GROOVE (TYP)
#6 × ³/₄″ LG FHWS
¹/₄″
¹/₄″
¹/₂″

BOTTOM JOINERY AND KICKER DETAIL

KICKER ON TOP DRAWERS ONLY
10⁷/₈″
¹/₂″
4¹⁵/₁₆″

FRONT VIEW
TOP DRAWER

10⁷/₈″
6³/₁₆″

FRONT VIEW
LOWER MIDDLE DRAWER

10⁷/₈″
5¹⁵/₁₆″

FRONT VIEW
UPPER MIDDLE DRAWER

10⁷/₈″
7³/₁₆″

FRONT VIEW
BOTTOM DRAWER

MAKING AND ATTACHING THE FEET AND THE APPLIQUÉS

You can adjust the style of a built-in by changing the doors, drawer faces, and moldings. And as I explained earlier, cabinetmakers have recently begun to experiment with appliqués — decorative parts attached directly to the surface of the cabinet — to change the look.

The bathroom vanity sports several of these appliqués. The split turnings at the front corners, and the rails and stiles on the sides are strictly ornamental; they have no structural function.

The vanity also has feet, parts not normally found on a built-in. Typically, a cabinet such as this would sit on its base (like the mission bookcase) or a *plinth,* a frame base beneath the case. But Mary Jane reduced the size of the plinth, making the feet functional as well as decorative.

TURNING THE FEET Turn the feet with ¾-inch-diameter tenons at the top, as shown in the *Foot Layout* on the facing page. Glue mounting blocks to the bottom of the case at the back corners, then drill ¾-inch-diameter mortises at all four corners. Glue the leg tenons in the mortises.

MAKING A SPLIT TURNING Jim turned the appliqués at the corners of the vanity as a single part, then split it in half. It's a neat trick and not

RESOURCES

Most mail-order woodworking supply companies carry some appliqués. The Woodworkers' Store has an unusually large selection. Their address is:

   The Woodworkers' Store
   4365 Willow Drive
   Medina, MN 55340

hard to do — just glue up two pieces of turning stock with a sheet of newspaper between the two. After turning the shape, drive a chisel into the glue joint. The two parts will separate cleanly. Then glue the split turning to the face frame.

MAKING FAUX RAILS AND STILES The sides are framed with thin strips glued directly to the surface, as shown in the *Side Trim Layout* on the facing page. This makes the sides look as if they were frame-and-panel construction. However, the rails and stiles in this construction are *faux* (false), just for show.

After turning and sanding the shape, drive a chisel into the glue seam at several locations. Just tap the chisel; you shouldn't have to drive it very hard. The piece of paper in the seam will enable the halves of the turning to split cleanly and evenly. To remove the paper, saturate it with water, then scrape it away with a putty knife.

TURNING BLOCKS

PAPER

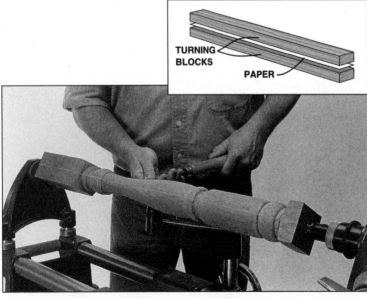

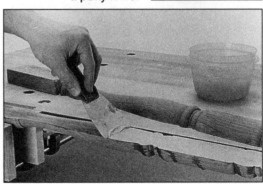

To make a split turning, glue two turning blocks face to face with a sheet of newspaper or Kraft paper between them. Let the glue dry for *at least* 24 hours, then turn the assembly as you would normally.

CONSIDER THIS!

Depending on the appliqué and where it's applied, it may make more sense to make and attach the part earlier in the project. For example, Jim and I found out the hard way that it would have been easier to glue the faux rails and stiles to the sides before the case was assembled.

MAKING A COUNTERTOP

A laminated countertop consists of a thin sheet of plastic laminate glued to a thick core or underlayment. Most cabinetmakers prefer to use either plywood or particleboard for the underlayment, often building up several layers to make a thick, strong base. The counter on this vanity is just a single thickness of particleboard covered with laminate.

Cut the counter, backsplash, and sidesplash cores, and cover them with laminate *before* you assemble them. It becomes much too difficult to apply laminate to the parts once they're joined.

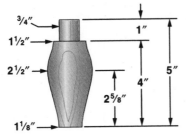

FOOT LAYOUT

FRONT CORNER SECTION

FALSE STILE
FRONT STILE
BOTTOM
FOOT

BACK CORNER SECTION

BOTTOM
BACK
BLOCK
FOOT

BOTTOM VIEW
FRONT CORNER

BOTTOM VIEW
BACK CORNER

¾" DIA ×
1" DP
HOLE

¾" THK ×
1½" WD ×
2¼" WD
BLOCK

SIDE TRIM LAYOUT

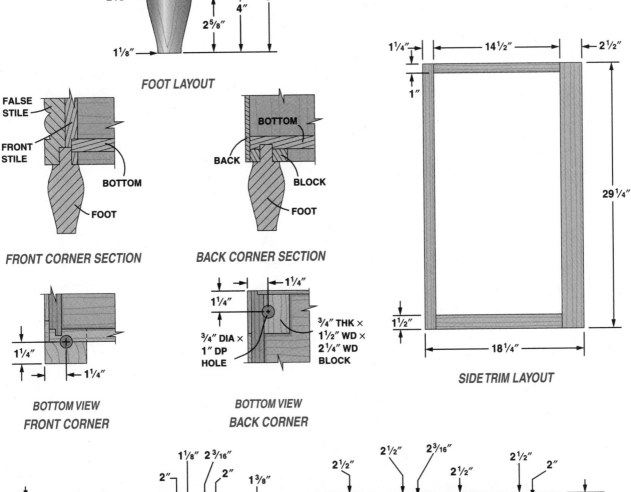

TURNING LAYOUT

The rule of thumb is to cover the vertical surfaces first, then the horizontal surfaces. That way, the horizontal laminate covers the edge of the vertical laminate the way a roof covers the walls of a house. Water is less likely to soak into the seam.

On the countertop, cover the edges first, then the surface. For the backsplash and sidesplashes, cover the faces, the ends, the angled edges, and the top edges, in that order.

Once the underlayment is covered with laminate, assemble the parts with silicone caulk. Clean up any squeeze-out with mineral spirits. Let the silicone set up overnight, then reinforce the joints by driving a screw up through the counter and into the backsplash and sidesplash. Also drive screws through the back of the backsplash and into the edges of the sidesplashes.

INSTALLING A BUILT-IN CABINET

Because this piece will probably be doused with water from time to time, apply a water-resistant finish, inside and out. Set the cabinet in place in your bathroom, and secure it to the wall. Attach the

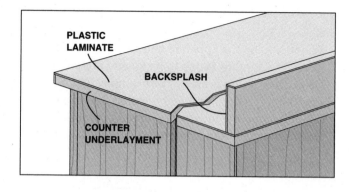

counter and set the sink in the counter. After installing the plumbing, slide the base frame into place and drive screws down through the bottom to hold it in place.

Look Here! For more information on installing a built-in cabinet, see page 50.

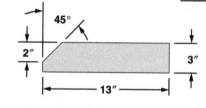

SPLASH GUARD LAYOUT

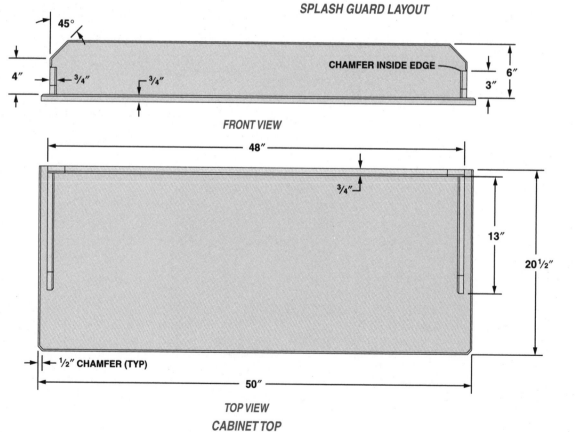

FRONT VIEW

TOP VIEW
CABINET TOP

METHODS OF WORK ■ *Applying Plastic Laminate*

Cut the plastic laminate 1 to 2 inches oversized by either sawing it on a table saw, cutting it with a router (guided by a straightedge), or scoring it with a scoring knife and breaking it along the score marks.

Apply contact cement to both the underlayment and the back side of the laminate. Let the cement dry until it's no longer tacky, then press it in place. Trim the laminate to the adjacent surfaces with a flush-trim router bit.

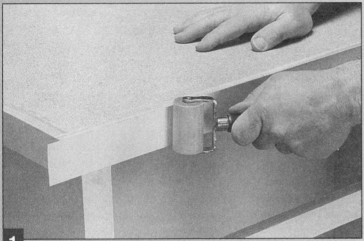

1 **Begin with the vertical surfaces.** On a counter, these would be the edges. Cut strips (called *self edges*) to cover the edges, apply cement, and let them dry. Press them in place, starting at one end and working toward the other. To get a good bond, apply additional pressure with a veneer roller.

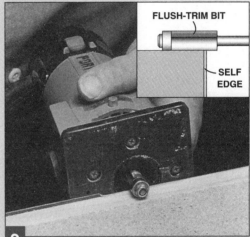

2 **Trim the portion** of the self edges that overhangs the surfaces using a router and a flush-trim bit. This cuts a square edge on the laminate.

3 **Next, cover the top surface** of the counter. Apply cement to the laminate and let it dry. Lay strips of wood or paper over the core and lay the laminate over the strips. The strips keep the laminate from bonding immediately while you adjust its position. Once the laminate is where you want it, remove the strips and press it in place. To generate enough pressure for a good bond, place a block of wood over the laminate to protect it and pound it with a mallet. Pound the entire surface.

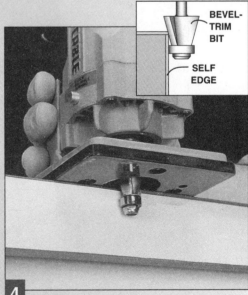

4 **Trim the overhang** with a bevel-trim bit. This cuts the laminate to size and bevels the edge at a slight angle. A beveled edge feels softer and won't chip as easily. For an even softer edge, *lightly* file the arris with a fine flat mill file, rounding it over slightly.

Joint Maker

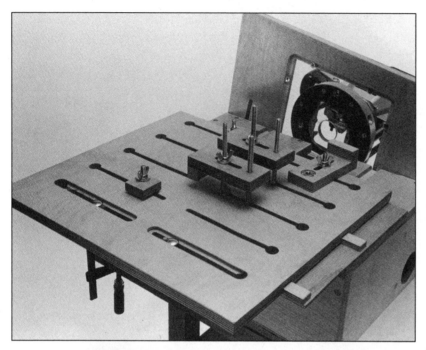

Holds router beside work

Easy height adjustment

Carriage and guides feed the work

Stops position the work and control the cut

Keyhole slots let you position clamps and stops quickly

Includes dust collection port

A horizontal routing jig, or *joint maker*, holds the router to one side of the work. This setup offers several advantages over a router table for certain operations. For example, you have more control when making mortises — you can rest the part on its face and feed the edge into the bit. When making tenons, the rotation of the bit doesn't pull the work sideways as it does on an ordinary router table. Instead, you cut directly against the rotation. And if you use vertical panel-raising bits, you'll find that with the panel resting flat on the work table, gravity works for you.

I've built several joint makers over the years and have noticed that this jig's most serious limitation is in routing small, narrow parts. Your hands come too close to the bit for safe, accurate control. So Jim and I added a *carriage* on this go-around, and it works wonderfully. Just clamp the part to the carriage and use the carriage to feed it into the router bit. Four stops on the carriage help position the work and control the cut. A unique *cross slide* (our invention!) keeps the work perfectly aligned with the bit yet allows you to feed it front-to-back or side-to-side.

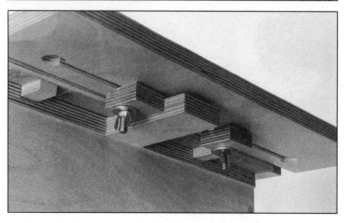

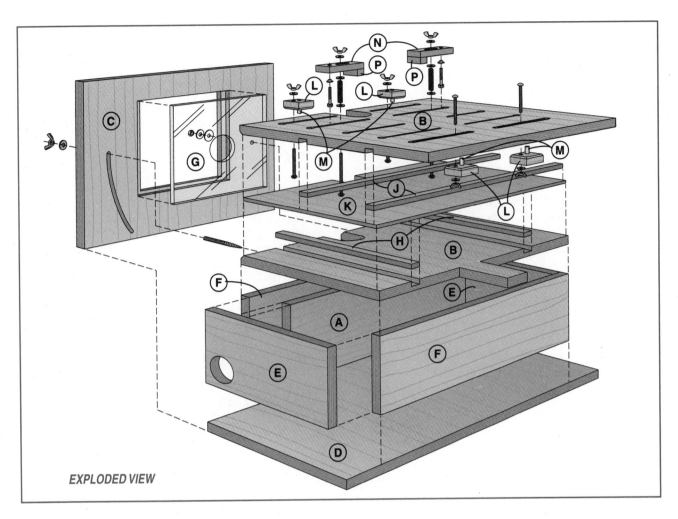

EXPLODED VIEW

JOINT MAKER ■ MATERIALS LIST

PARTS

A	Baffle	¾" x 6" x 16½"
B	Top/carriage (2)	¾" x 16" x 18"
C	Router mount	¾" x 13¾" x 18"
D	Bottom	¾" x 12" x 24"
E	Ends (2)	¾" x 6" x 10½"
F	Sides (2)	¾" x 6" x 18"
G	Router mounting plate*	⅜" x 8¾" x 8¾"
H	Front-to-back slides (2)	¼" x ¾" x 11¾"
J	Side-to-side slides (2)	¼" x ¾" x 18"
K	Cross slide mount	¼" x 11¾" x 18"
L	Stops‡ (4)	¾" x 1½" x 1½"
M	Stop pins (4)	5⁄16" dia. x 1"
N	Clamps (3)	¾" x 2" x 5¾"
P	Clamp jaws (3)	¾" x ¾" x 2"

* Make this part from acrylic plastic.

‡ Make this part from hardwood.

HARDWARE

5⁄16" x 2" Carriage bolts (6)	
5⁄16" x 5" Carriage bolts (3)	
5⁄16" Flat washers (15)	
5⁄16" Wing nuts (8)	
5⁄16" Fender washer	
5⁄16" Stop nut	
#10 x ¾" Flathead sheet metal screws (8) & nuts	
#12 x 1½" Flathead wood screw	
#8 x 1¾" Flathead wood screws (45)	
5⁄16" x 4" Full-thread hex bolts (3)	
5⁄16" T-nuts (3)	
Compression springs (3)	.030 wire x 11⁄32" I.D. x 5" lg.
5⁄16" x 3" Hanger bolt	
150-grit PSA Sandpaper	

How do I build it?

In essence, the joint maker is just a Baltic (European) birch plywood box with two flat work surfaces — one vertical, the other horizontal — mounted to it. The vertical surface, or *router mount,* is attached to the back of the box and holds the router. The horizontal surface, or *carriage,* slides over the top of the box and holds the work.

Cut the parts to the sizes given in the Materials List. Rout ¾-inch-wide, ¼-inch-deep grooves in the top surface of the top, as shown in the *Top Layout–Top View,* and the bottom surface of the carriage, as shown in the *Carriage Layout–Bottom View* on the facing page. Note that the grooves in the top run front-to-back, while those in the carriage run side-to-side. These grooves fit the cross slides.

Cut the shape of the top and cross slide mount. The top has a "fixed stop" on one side and a cutout in the other, as shown in the *Top Layout–Top View.*

Cut a 2¼-inch-diameter dust collection hole in one end, as shown in the *Side View.* And finally, drill a 5⁄16-inch-diameter pivot hole for the router mount in the back side, as shown in the *Back View.*

Assemble the bottom, sides, ends, and baffle with glue and screws. Insert the carriage bolt that serves as the pivot for the router mount through the pivot hole in the back side, then screw the top in place. However, *don't* glue it to the assembly. Jim and I found that out the hard way. If the pivot bolt happens to fall out, you can lose your religion trying to get it back in. (Of course, had we been smart, we would have epoxied the bolt in place.)

MOUNTING THE ROUTER

Jim attached the router to a clear plastic plate and then mounted the plate in the router mount. Because the mounting plate is thinner than the board to which it's attached, this arrangement gives you a fraction of an inch more depth of cut. More important, it lets you see what the router is doing as you cut.

Make a cutout, and rabbet the edge to accept the mounting plate. Attach the plate to the mount with #10 flathead sheet metal screws. When installed, the mounting plate must be flush with the work surface of the router mount. The heads of the screws must be countersunk in the plastic mounting plate so they rest slightly below the surface.

First use the plastic mounting plate itself as a template when making the rabbeted cutout. Position the plate on the mount where you want to attach it. Using double-faced carpet tape, attach wood strips around the perimeter of the plate to make a frame. The wood strips must be 1½ inches wide and as tall as the cutting flutes plus the bearing height.

Then remove the plate from inside the frame. With a router and a ¾-inch pattern-cutting bit, cut a ¾-inch-wide groove in the mount, following the inside edge of the frame with the pilot bearing on the bit. The completed groove should be roughly square. Its depth must be equal to the thickness of the plate.

Finally remove the frame and cut out the waste from inside the center of the square groove, using a scroll saw or saber saw. As you cut away the inside, the groove will become a ⅜-inch-wide rabbet. Secure the mounting plate in the rabbet with countersunk sheet metal screws and nuts.

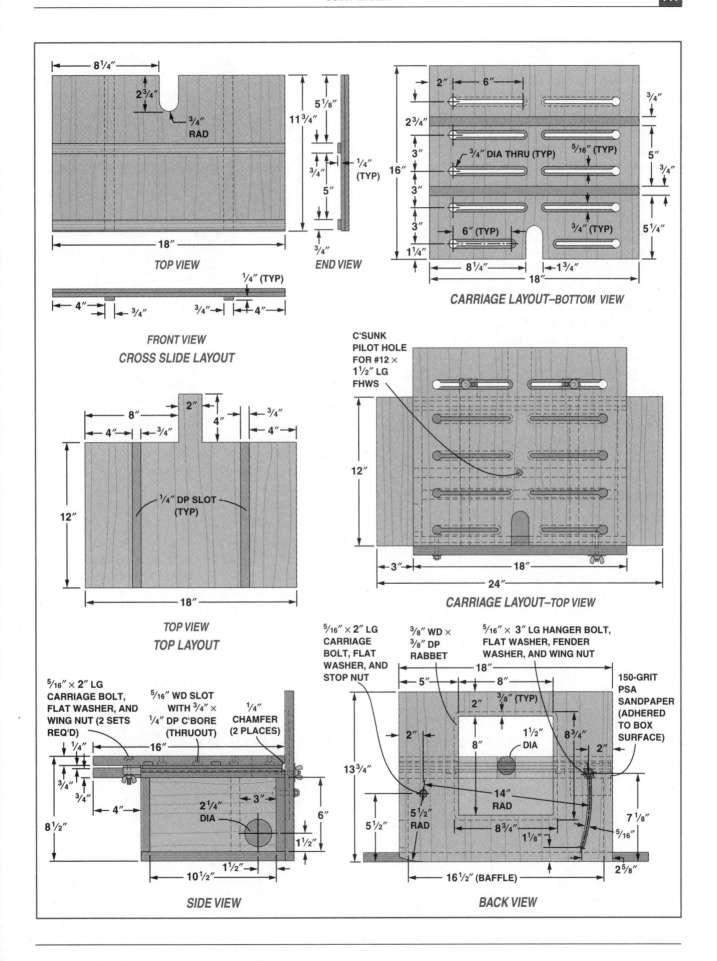

TOP VIEW

8¼"

2¾"

¾" RAD

5⅛"

11¾"

¾"

5"

¾"

¼" (TYP)

18"

END VIEW

¼" (TYP)

4"   ¾"   ¾"   4"

FRONT VIEW
CROSS SLIDE LAYOUT

2"

2¾"

16"

3"

3"

3"

3"

1¼"

6"

2"

6"

¾" DIA THRU (TYP)

5/16" (TYP)

¾"

5"

¾"

6" (TYP)

¾" (TYP)

5¼"

8¼"

1¾"

18"

CARRIAGE LAYOUT–BOTTOM VIEW

8"

2"

4"

¾"

¾"

4"

4"

¼" DP SLOT (TYP)

12"

18"

TOP VIEW
TOP LAYOUT

C'SUNK
PILOT HOLE
FOR #12 ×
1½" LG
FHWS

12"

3"

18"

24"

CARRIAGE LAYOUT–TOP VIEW

5/16" × 2" LG
CARRIAGE BOLT,
FLAT WASHER, AND
WING NUT (2 SETS
REQ'D)

5/16" WD SLOT
WITH ¾" ×
¼" DP C'BORE
(THRUOUT)

¼"
CHAMFER
(2 PLACES)

¼"

¾"

¾"

8½"

16"

4"

2¼"
DIA

3"

6"

1½"

10½"

1½"

SIDE VIEW

5/16" × 2" LG
CARRIAGE
BOLT, FLAT
WASHER, AND
STOP NUT

⅜" WD ×
⅜" DP
RABBET

5/16" × 3" LG HANGER BOLT,
FLAT WASHER, FENDER
WASHER, AND WING NUT

150-GRIT
PSA
SANDPAPER
(ADHERED
TO BOX
SURFACE)

18"

5"

8"

2"

⅜" (TYP)

2"

8"

1½"
DIA

8¾"

2"

13¾"

5½"
RAD

14"
RAD

8¾"

1⅛"

5/16"

7⅛"

2⅝"

16½" (BAFFLE)

BACK VIEW

CUTTING THE SLOTS

There are two types of slots in this fixture. The carriage has several *keyhole* slots — straight slots with a ¾-inch-diameter hole at one end, as shown in the *Carriage Layout–Bottom View* on page 117. The holes let you mount the stops and clamps instantly, without having to remove the hardware — just insert the heads of the mounting bolts in the holes and slide the stop sideways in the slot. The slots let you position the stops and clamps wherever you need them. Note that these slots are *counterbored,* as shown in the *Side View* on page 117. (A cross section of the slot looks like an inverted T.) The counterbores hold the heads of the bolts so they don't rub on the top of the fixture.

To make the keyhole slots, drill the ¾-inch-diameter holes *first*. Then rout ¾-inch-wide, ¼-inch-deep counterbore grooves, using the T-Square Router Guide (page 13) to guide the router. Without changing the position of the router guide, change bits and rout a ⁵⁄₁₆-inch-wide slot through the middle of each groove.

To rout the curved slot in the router mount, attach the router to a router compass jig, as shown below. This serves as a compass. Insert a pivot bolt through the compass and the mount, then swing the router in an arc as you cut.

ASSEMBLING THE CROSS SLIDE

The cross slide is a simple assembly, but you have to get all four of the slides positioned correctly for it to work well. Jim found that the best way to do this was to use the tool itself as a glue-up jig.

Make a counterbored slot in two steps (Photos show a lengthwise cross-section of a slot). First rout the wide "counterbore groove" that forms the step inside the slots *(top).* Then rout a slot down the middle of the groove, cutting completely through the stock in four ⅛"-deep passes *(bottom).*

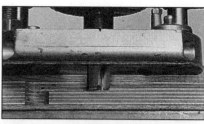

Place a single layer of thin plastic in the grooves in both the top and the carriage. (Jim used a plastic grocery bag because it was the thinnest plastic he could find.) Then press the slides into their grooves on top of the plastic. Apply a thin bead of glue to the exposed surface of each slide. Place the cross slide mount on top of the slides in the top, then place the carriage (with the slides in place) on top of it. Don't worry if there's a little glue squeeze-out; the plastic will prevent it from accidentally bonding surfaces that it shouldn't.

Make sure that everything lines up properly and that the back edge of the carriage is flush with the back of the joint maker. Then clamp the parts together and let the glue dry. After it sets up, take the carriage, cross slide, and joint maker apart, and discard the plastic.

DRILL TO FIT SCREWS AND HOLE PATTERN OF ROUTER BASE.

RADIUS TO FIT ROUTER BASE

DRILL PIVOT HOLES ANYWHERE ALONG CENTERLINE.

14"

1" DIA HOLE

1" RAD

⁵⁄₁₆" DIA HOLE

¼" PLYWOOD OR HARDBOARD

ROUTER COMPASS JIG

To rout the curved slot in the router mount, first make a router compass jig to guide your router in an arc. Drill the ⁵⁄₁₆-inch-diameter mounting hole in the router mount and mark the ends of the curved slot. Attach your router to the compass jig and, using the mounting hole as the pivot, swing the router in an arc to cut the slot.

MAKING THE STOPS AND CLAMPS

Both the stops and the clamps are attached to the carriage with carriage bolts. The stops are blocks of wood with dowels protruding from the underside to keep them from rotating when in use. Chamfers around the bottom edges prevent the sawdust from interfering with the accuracy of the setup. Jim and I have found that as sawdust builds up around the stops, it prevents the parts from making full contact. This, in turn, keeps you from positioning the parts correctly. The chamfers give the sawdust somewhere to go. You still have to brush the dust away from time to time, but you don't have to get every little particle.

On the clamps, a compression spring around the mounting bolt automatically raises the clamp when you loosen the knob. A hex bolt threaded into a T-nut at the back of the clamp prevents the assembly from tipping when you apply pressure.

Make as many clamps and stops as you think you'll need. Jim made just three clamps and four stops, and I've found those adequate for the work we do. But if you think you'll need more, now's the time to make them.

FINAL ASSEMBLY AND FINISHING

Give all the wooden surfaces a light sanding, then apply a durable finish to the joint maker, router mount, carriage, cross slide, clamps, and stops. I usually mix spar varnish and tung oil half-and-half for this job. Apply a thin coat to all exposed surfaces, then rub down those surfaces that will slide together — such as the back and the router mount, or the top and the cross slide — with steel wool or fine abrasive pads. Then apply a coat of paste furniture wax to the sliding surfaces of the top, cross slide, and carriage, and *buff it out*. The thin layer of wax lubricates the surfaces and helps the parts slide easily.

Attach the router mount to the joint maker with a pivot bolt, washer, and a stop nut. Using the curved slot as a guide, drill a ¼-inch-diameter pilot hole for the hanger bolt in the edge of the top. Install the hanger bolt, fender washer, flat washer, and wing nut, as shown in the *Back View* (page 117). Also install the hardware in the stops and clamps. The carriage and cross slide are not attached; they simply rest on top of the joint maker.

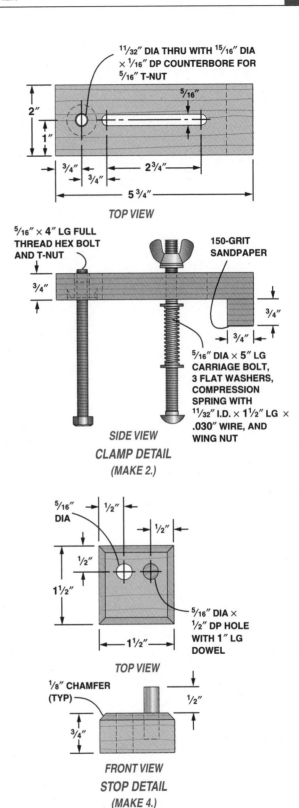

Note: For some operations, you will need the carriage to remain stationary. To lock it in place, drive a #12 flathead wood screw through the carriage, cross slide, and top, as shown in *Carriage Layout–Top View* on page 117.

METHODS OF WORK ■ *Using the Joint Maker*

Perhaps one of the best ways to illustrate how to use this tool is to walk you through a joint. Remember the haunched mortise and tenon that we used to join the frame-and-panel door on the spice cupboard? On page 21, I showed you how to make that particular joint on a table saw and a drill press. With the joint maker, however, you can do it all on one machine.

1 **Begin by cutting** the grooves in the inside edges of the rails and stiles. Mount a straight bit in the router, and adjust the depth of cut so the bit protrudes from the mounting plate. Lock the carriage to the base with a #12 flathead wood screw. To adjust the position of the groove in the edge, raise or lower the router by pivoting the mount then locking it down. Feed the parts past the bit, guiding them along the mount.

2 **Clamp a stile** to the carriage so the inside (grooved) edge faces the router. Adjust the hex bolts so the clamp jaws sit squarely on the work while you tighten down the knobs.

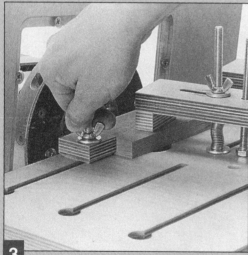

3 **Secure a stop** against the end of the stile — this will help you quickly align the other stiles. Calculate how long you want to cut the mortises, and position two more adjustable stops to contact the top's protruding fixed stop at the beginning and end of each cut.

4 **Advance the router bit** to cut the full depth of the mortise. Holding onto the carriage, feed the stock into the bit no more than 1/8 inch. Move it side to side, cutting the full length of the mortise. Then feed it another 1/8 inch into the bit and repeat. Continue until you have cut the mortise to the desired depth. **Note: To cut through mortises in wide stiles, work from *both* edges of the board. Cut as deep as you can in the first edge. Then, keeping the same face on the carriage, turn the board and cut the other edge. The two cuts will join to make a single mortise.**

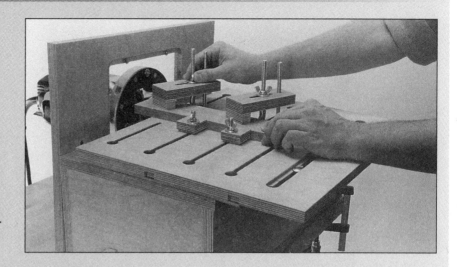

5 **Mount a rail** on the carriage so the edge is perpendicular to the router mount. Once again, secure stops against the rail to help you position the others for duplicate cuts. **Note: You may need a backup board to prevent tear-out.**

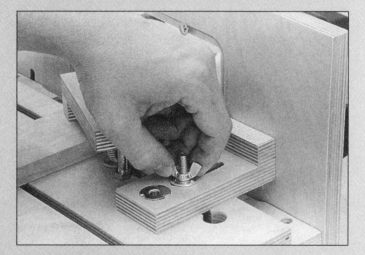

6 **Using the wooden clamp** as a stop, attach it to the carriage and position it to limit the carriage travel. This will prevent the bit from cutting into the carriage as you work. Adjust the height of the bit to cut the *underside* of the stock.

7 **Cut the tenons** in the ends of each rail. To make each cheek, feed the rail across the bit, guiding the carriage stop against the router mount. Loosen the clamps, turn the rail face for face, and make a second cheek.

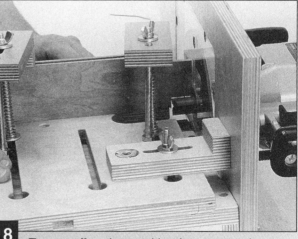

8 **Turn a rail** so the *outside* edge rests on the carriage, and clamp it in place. Readjust the router bit and cut the haunch in the tenon. For all of these operations, use the carriage to feed the work and to control the cut.

Index

A few essential woodworking secrets...

Dress for success.

■ Always wear eye protection — safety glasses for most operations, a full face shield for turning, routing, and other operations that throw wood chips. Always presume that every board you cut has a splinter with your name on it.

■ Wear a dust mask when sanding and sawing — sawdust (especially fine sawdust) may be harmful to your lungs.

■ Wear hearing protectors when routing or planing and for long, continuous power-tool operations. The high frequencies can harm your ears.

■ Wear rubber gloves when handling dangerous chemicals — many of these can harm your skin or can be absorbed through the skin.

■ Wear a vapor mask when finishing — the vapors of some finishing chemicals are potentially toxic.

■ Wear close-fitting clothes with the sleeves rolled up above the elbows. Remove jewelry or anything that might catch on a tool.

Work smart.

■ Install good lighting — it helps to see what you're doing.

■ Hang or store tools within easy reach — the work goes faster.

■ Keep your work area free of clutter — you don't want to trip when surrounded by sharp tools.

■ Install a circuit breaker box within easy reach, and make sure each circuit is grounded and rated for sufficient amperage.

■ Keep blades and cutters sharp and free of pitch — a dull tool is harder to control and therefore more dangerous than a sharp one.

■ Keep arbors, tables, and fences properly aligned — misaligned tools are an accident waiting to happen.

■ Keep tables and fences waxed and rust-free — this gives you more control over your work.

■ Store flammable chemicals in fireproof containers. The same goes for shop rags. Some finishes generate heat as they cure and may cause rags to combust spontaneously.

Work safe.

■ Keep the blade and cutter guards in place. They're like seat belts — they're a bother at first, but pretty soon you will feel uncomfortable without them.

■ Mark the danger zones around blades and cutters, and keep your hands and fingers out of these areas.